Asian Fusion

Chat Mingkwan

Book Publishing Company
Summertown, Tennessee

© 2010 Chat Mingkwan

Photos © 2010 Book Publishing Company

Cover design: Warren Jefferson
Interior design: Publishers' Design and Production Services
Cover and interior photos: Warren Jefferson
Food styling: Barbara Jefferson

Cover photo - Filipino Pancit Noodles (Pancit Guisado), p. 121

Book Publishing Company   ISBN: 978-1-57067-231-6
P.O. Box 99
Summertown, TN 38483   17 16 15 14 13 12 11 10   9 8 7 6 5 4 3 2 1
888-260-8458
www.bookpubco.com   Printed in Canada

Library of Congress Cataloging-in-Publication Data

Chat Mingkwan.
    Asian fusion / by Chat Mingkwan.
        p. cm.
    Includes bibliographical references and index.
    Summary: "In Asian Fusion, Chat Mingkwan presents faithful vegetarian translations of signature dishes
from all corners of the Asian continent. Readers will get information on how to use and where to find
herbs and spices unique to this area and will enjoy Chat's practical approach to creating authentic Asian
flavors in Western kitchens"—Provided by publisher.
    ISBN 978-1-57067-231-6 (alk. paper)
    1. Cooking, Asian. 2. Vegetarian cooking. I. Title.
    TX724.5.A1C44 2010
    641.595—dc22
                                2010021654

Book Publishing Company is a member of Green Press Initiative. We chose to print this title on paper with
postconsumer recycled content, processed without chlorine, which saved the following natural resorces:

60 trees
1,662 pounds of solid waste
27,367 gallons of water
5,682 pounds of greenhouse gasses
19 million BTU of energy

For more information about Green Press Initiative, visit www.greenpressinitiative.com.
Environmental impact estimates were made using the Environmental Defense Fund Paper Calculator.
For more information, visit www.papercalculator.org.

Contents

Though you've been a vital part of me, even a small fraction of what you do can often take my breath away. And thanks for being a part of this book.

A portion of the proceeds from this book will be donated to projects that promote the preservation of endangered wildlife. With your help, they'll keep on roaming.

Preface

In my first vegetarian cookbook, *Buddha's Table: Thai Feasting Vegetarian Style*, I vowed to convert recipes from cuisines around the world to vegetarian. This task is enormous, especially because I want to maintain the native essence of each cuisine while encouraging vegetarians as well as nonvegetarians to give new foods a try. I have kept my vow thus far, and it resulted in my second vegetarian cookbook, *Vietnamese Fusion*.

My teaching curriculum has been incredibly well received, and my cooking classes have been packed with vegetarian students seeking to acquire new understanding of Thai and Vietnamese cuisine. With all this support in my cooking classes and encouragement from the sale of both books, I have continued to convert recipes, spreading my geographic focus to all parts of Asia, including Burma, China, Philippines, India, Indonesia, Japan, Korea, Laos, Malaysia, Singapore, Sri Lanka, Thailand, and Vietnam. I have tried new recipes, learned how to use (and pronounce) new ingredients, and discovered how to use familiar ingredients in exciting new ways. I share all of that with you here in this book.

I appreciate your support and encouragement in my vegetarian endeavors, and I have extended the same courtesy to others who seek a health-promoting and environmentally supportive lifestyle.

Thank you.
Arigato.
Cam on.
Chezu ba.
Kamapsumida.
Khawp jai.
Khawp khun.
Salamut.
Shukriya.
Terima kasik.
Xie xie.

Chat Mingkwan

Introduction

It has been my lifelong dream to travel and eat my way through all parts of Asia, enjoying the gastronomic changes from one border to another. I have not yet fulfilled that dream. However, I have made culinary hops from one place to another, enjoying great food, the cordiality of the local people, and breathtaking scenery.

As there was no chronological order to my trips, it is difficult to differentiate among or sum up the various Asian cuisines, so I have had to rely on my memories and notes from my past trips in combination with my research on each cuisine. Since ancient times, India and China have been Asian powerhouses and exuded their influences throughout Asia. For example, Indian curries and Chinese stir-fries are more or less present in all Asian cuisines. Indonesian *sambal*, a spicy-hot condiment, has an Indian touch, and *nasi goreng* (fried rice) and Filipino *pancit* noodles have a Chinese touch.

When the seaports in Asia opened to international fleets, the Portuguese and Spanish voyagers reached Asia first, followed by the British, Dutch, French, and others who established their trading depots and companies. Inevitably, the European influence spread through the local cuisines, as reflected in Portuguese-inspired Japanese tempura, French-inspired Vietnamese crêpes, Spanish-inspired Filipino *guisado* (stew), and Dutch-inspired Indonesian *kecap manis* (thick, sweet soy sauce).

During the process of integrating foreign influences, the native people asserted their own personalities by using local ingredients and flavors to suit their palates, evolving many Asian cuisines with a unique set of characteristics. Besides the Indian and Chinese influences, which are the tour de force of Asian cuisine, Japanese food is by far the most unique, with its centuries of "closed-door" evolution that brought us sushi and *kaiseki* (a traditional multicourse meal), followed by Korean food, with its numerous small-plated accompaniments and *kimchi*. Vietnamese cuisine, with its healthful approach and one-of-a-kind fresh herbs, such as *rau ram* and *ngo gai*, has recently become popular. Thai cuisine represents the bold and bright flavor of sweet-sour-hot, which is created with Thai chiles, lemongrass, galangal, and kaffir lime. Malaysian and Indonesian cuisines infuse their native specialties with local products from the Spice Islands. Singaporean food exemplifies a blend of Asian cuisines, where Chinese, Indian, and Malaysian fare coexist harmoniously in the local meals.

Asian cuisines have many similarities that their histories help explain, but they also have subtle differences as distinctive as sweet and bitter that connoisseurs appreciate and respect. Capturing the exciting flair and flavor of these fascinating cuisines can be done with minimal effort. I encourage all vegetarians to give Asian cooking a try!

Special Ingredients

Asian cooking uses a wide range of ingredients derived from different climates, landscapes, and methods of harvesting and processing. Some parts of Asia use coconut for sweetness instead of sugar, tamarind for a sour taste instead of lemon or lime, and spicy chiles for heat instead of ground pepper. Some of the ingredients are new to Western kitchens, even though they are accessible through Asian markets in the United States.

The majority of Asian cuisines use some animal-based seasonings, such as fish sauce in Thai and Vietnamese cuisines, primarily because of its saltiness and value as a flavor enhancer. Other exotic ingredients, such as shrimp paste and fermented fish, also add authentic flavors. But none of these products are vegetarian. Therefore, various plant-based seasoning are used instead.

Don't be put off by unfamiliar ingredients and techniques. Asian cooking is not a difficult or complicated process. In fact, by becoming familiar with the ingredients and their uses, lovers of Asian food can easily prepare any dish from any menu.

Soy Products

Soybeans are used to produce a wide range of products used extensively in Asian cuisine. The Chinese have cultivated soybeans for centuries, dating back to 2838 BC. In China, they are considered one of the five sacred grains, *wu lu*. The United States has now become the largest producer of soybeans, supplying about 75 percent of the world's total production. There are more than one thousand varieties, ranging in size from a small pea to a large cherry. The beans come in various colors and combinations of red, yellow, green, brown, and black. Unlike other legumes, the soybean is low in carbohydrates and high in protein.

Bean sauce and **bean paste** are seasonings made from fermented soybeans. They can range from thin to thick and from smooth to chunky. They should be stored in a nonmetallic, tightly sealed container in the refrigerator, where they will keep for up to a year.

Black bean sauce is a thin, salty, full-flavored mixture made with mashed fermented black beans and flavored with garlic and sometimes star anise.

Brown bean sauce, or *fermented yellow bean sauce*, is thick and made with fermented whole yellow soybeans, salt, and water.

Fermented black beans, also known as Chinese black beans or salty black beans, are a Chinese specialty consisting of small black soybeans that have been preserved in salt before being packed into cans or plastic bags. They have an extremely pungent, salty flavor and must be soaked in warm water for about thirty minutes before using.

Fermented yellow beans are whole yellow soybeans that have been fermented in water and salt. They often come in a bottle and are ready to be used in stir-fries and sauces.

Hot black bean sauce has a medium consistency and is a combination of black soybeans, chiles, garlic, sesame oil, and sugar.

Miso, a fermented soybean paste, is essential in Japanese cooking. The three most common varieties are barley miso, rice miso, and soybean miso. Each has different flavor, color, and salt content, and some may have added sugar. Miso can be used in sauces, soups, marinades, main dishes, and salad dressings.

Sweet bean paste is made from fermented soybeans and sugar. It is quite thick and has a sweet-salty flavor.

Soymilk is a protein-rich, cholesterol-free, nondairy liquid made by pressing ground, cooked soybeans. Soymilk has a tendency to curdle when mixed with acidic ingredients, such as lemon juice or wine. It is an important ingredient in making tofu.

Soy sauce is a dark, salty sauce made with fermented, boiled soybeans and roasted wheat or barley. China and Japan produce a number of varieties ranging in color from light to dark and in texture from thin to very thick.

Dark soy sauce refers to "regular" soy sauce. It has a rich soy flavor and color. This soy sauce is generally used when a particular type is not specified in the recipe.

Double-dark soy sauce is a lot darker than regular soy sauce and is used mostly for glazing or for sauces that need a dark brown color.

Light soy sauce is much thinner and lighter than regular dark soy sauce. It is also called "cooking soy sauce," as it has less soy flavor and a lighter color that won't turn sauces dark brown. It is sometimes marketed as "thin soy sauce" or "white soy sauce"; they are all the same product. Light soy sauce is the best substitute for fish sauce in a vegetarian dish.

Lite soy sauce is regular soy sauce with less sodium.

Seasoning soy sauce is a soy sauce with natural flavor enhancers added. It helps improve the flavor of a dish and adds depth beyond regular soy sauce. Some seasoning soy sauces are made with mushrooms and seaweeds. One popular brand-name product is Maggi Seasoning Sauce. Others may be marketed as mushroom-flavored soy sauce or all-purpose seasoning soy sauce.

Sushi, or *sashimi soy sauce*, is a milder soy sauce with added rice products to sweeten its taste. It is more expensive than regular soy sauce and often is used as a dipping sauce.

Sweet soy sauce is a thick, sweet, dark sauce made from soy sauce and molasses or palm sugar. It often is used instead of sugar and is valued for its dark color, thick consistency, and sweetness.

Tamari is the Japanese dark soy sauce. It is rich, thick, and extremely dark.

Tofu (bean curd) is made from curdled soymilk, resulting in curds that are drained and pressed in a fashion similar to making cheese. Tofu has a bland, slightly nutty flavor that easily takes on the flavor of the food it's cooked with. Tofu comes in regular, low-fat, and nonfat varieties and in textures ranging from soft to extra firm.

Baked tofu is tofu that has been baked, seasoned, and sealed in a package. Baking rids the tofu of excess moisture, making it drier and firmer, and infuses it with intense flavor. It is often prepared with added spices, such as Chinese five-spice powder. Store it in the refrigerator for up to one week.

Fermented bean curds are tofu curds that have been fermented with salt, water, vinegar, rice wine, and/or spices until they develop an extremely pungent taste equivalent to Thai shrimp paste or Limburger cheese. They come in a small jar and should be stored tightly sealed in the refrigerator for up to one year.

Fried tofu is tofu that has been deep-fried and sealed in a package. It is somewhat crunchy on the outside and soft and smooth in the inside. It contains small air pockets that readily absorb sauces and flavors. Store it in the refrigerator for up to one week.

Pressed tofu is sold in small squares. It has a meaty, chewy texture and may have added coloring or flavorings.

Silken tofu is named for its silky smooth texture and comes in soft, firm, and extra-firm styles. It usually is packed in water and sold in a sealed plastic container, or it is vacuum-packed in plastic without water. Silken tofu is also available in aseptically sealed cartons that may be stored unopened at room temperature for up to eight months. Once opened, silken tofu should be covered with water, which should be changed daily, and stored in the refrigerator, where it will keep for five to seven days.

Tofu sheets, or *tofu skins*, are a thin layer of tofu that curdles on the surface of hot soymilk. They are sold three different ways: fresh, folded or rolled in a sealed plastic package and dried in a big sheet, or packed airtight in a plastic bag. Dried tofu sheets can be kept for up to one year and must be reconstituted before using. Fresh tofu sheets will keep for about one week in the refrigerator. Fresh or reconstituted dried tofu sheets can be cut to desired sizes and used as wrappers or added to soups and stir-fries.

Herbs and Spices

What makes each Asian cuisine unique are the special herbs and spices. Lemongrass, Thai sweet basil, and a variety of chiles have earned their shelf space in the big-name grocery stores. Though most Asian herbs and spices can be cultivated locally, some must be imported in various forms: fresh, dried, powdered, frozen, or canned in brine. For some herbs and spices, substitutions can easily be made by using items more readily available outside Asia. However, to maintain an authentic essence, the herbs and spices listed below with an asterisk (*) cannot be replaced.

Asafetida, also known as *hing*, is a spice that is widely used in Indian cuisine. When raw, it has a pungent, garlicky smell, but after being cooked, its aroma become milder and more pleasant, similar to leeks. Asafetida is usually sold in powder form at Indian grocery stores.

Basil is common to Asian cooking, and many different types are used. True basil is a member of the mint family, signified by its square stems. The "basil" used in some Asian cuisines, however, may not be in the mint family; instead, it has similar mint characteristics, such as Vietnamese *rau ram*. For this reason, it may be hard to find the exact basil to use. Feel free to alternate among them or just use Italian basil.

Holy basil, used in Thai cuisine, has a distinctive light reddish violet hue on both its leaves and stems. It imparts a mintlike zesty and spicy flavor and is used for stir-fries. Holy basil is hard to find and is mostly available during the midsummer months, when it thrives.

Lemon basil has light green leaves with a slight speckle of hairs, green stems, and sometimes white flowers. It has a nippy, peppery, lemon flavor that goes well with soups, salads, and especially curried noodles.

Thai sweet basil has small, flat green leaves with pointy tips, and its stems and flowers are sometimes reddish purple. It imparts a very intense taste with a strong anise or licorice flavor. It's often used as a flavorful garnish for coconut curries and leafy vegetables. Ordinary sweet basil makes a good substitute. Thai sweet basil is available year-round.

Cardamom* is indigenous to India and Sri Lanka. Cardamom has a eucalyptus-like lemony flavor and is essential to Indian curries. It is available as dried whole seeds or ground.

Chiles are very spicy, and for those used in Asian cuisine, the smallest are the hottest.

Asian chiles come in green, red, or yellow and are the size of a forefinger. They look similar to a jalape–o chile but with a pointy tip. They are a lot milder than Thai chiles and are used both fresh and dried. Fresh green chiles are used in green curry paste. Dried red chiles are used in red and yellow curry paste. If fresh Asian chiles are not available, use fresh serrano or jalape–o chiles. For the dried chiles, large dried Mexican chiles, such as guajillo chiles, California chiles, or New Mexico chiles, are good substitutes.

Serrano chiles are green chiles with smooth skins and round bodies. As they mature, their color changes from bright green to scarlet red and then yellow. They are easily found in markets in the United States. Their flavor is as mild as Asian chiles, making them a good multipurpose chile.

Thai chiles, or *bird's-eye chiles*, called *prik khee nu*, which literally means "mouse droppings" in Thai, are the smallest chiles. They are green, red, or yellow and have an extremely pungent taste. Thai chiles are used for chile sauces and dips and are added to curry pastes for spicy heat. They are available in most Asian grocery stores and are usually labeled "Thai chiles."

Chinese five-spice* is a Chinese ground spice mixture; it is sometimes labeled "five-fragrance powder." It is golden brown and consists of cassia (Asian cinnamon), cloves, fennel, star anise, and Szechuan pepper (or ginger and/or cardamom). The flavor of star anise is the strongest in the mixture.

Cilantro*, or **Chinese parsley**, is indispensable to Asian cooking and is used generously. Each part of the plant, from the roots to the leaves, can be used for different purposes. The roots and seeds (also known as coriander seeds) are very pungent and are important ingredients in curry pastes and for flavoring clear soup broths. The stems and leaves are used both for flavoring and as a leafy green garnish. Cilantro has delicate, light green leaves and stems, with white or light pink flowers; all of these parts are edible. In most supermarkets in the United States, cilantro is sold without roots, but the stems can be substituted for the roots in cooking. To enhance their aroma, coriander seeds should be dry roasted before being used in a recipe. Like any other dried spices, coriander seeds and ground coriander will lose their fragrance and flavor after six months.

Curry leaves* are the leaves of curry trees, native to India. The leaves are pinnate, with eleven to twenty-one leaflets, and each leaflet is about one and a half inches long and one inch wide. Fresh leaves are highly aromatic and used similarly to bay leaves in many South Indian and Sri Lankan dishes. Dried and frozen curry leaves can also be found in Asian grocery stores, but they are far inferior to the fresh leaves.

Fenugreek seeds* are rhombic, with a yellow to amber color and a bittersweet taste. The seeds are frequently used in the preparation of curry powder, curry pastes, and pickles. Young leaves and sprouts are eaten as greens, and the fresh and dried leaves are used to flavor other dishes. Fenugreek seeds can be found in the spice aisle of most grocery stores, especially Indian grocery stores.

Galangal*, also called **Siamese ginger**, is a perennial rhizome similar to ginger but with a larger and brighter colored root. The root tips are pink and have a strong medicinal taste, so they can't be eaten directly like ginger. Galangal is used as a pungent ingredient in ground curry pastes and contributes a unique taste and exotic aroma to the popular Thai hot-and-sour soup *tom kha*. Galangal can be found fresh, frozen, dried, and powdered in most Asian grocery stores. If you are using dried slices of galangal, soak them in warm water for at least thirty minutes, or until the pieces can be easily bent. Substitute fresh galangal for half the amount of dried galangal called for in a recipe. Regular ginger cannot duplicate the authentic essence of galangal. Only as a last resource should ginger ever be used instead of galangal.

Garam masala is an Indian blend of dry-roasted, ground spices, adding *garam*, which means "warmth" or "heat" to the palate. There are many varieties of garam masala, which vary according to local and regional tastes. Spices often include black pepper, cardamom, chiles, cinnamon, cloves, coriander, cumin, fennel, mace, nutmeg, and other spices. Garam masala can be purchased in Indian markets and in most supermarkets. It's also easily prepared at home. It should be stored, like other spices, in a cool, dry place for about six months.

Garlic chives, or **Chinese chives**, have a stronger aroma than European chives. They have long, flat, slender leaves and long stems topped with white flowers. They are used exclusively for stir-fried dishes and as a garnish over noodle dishes. Green onions are a good substitute.

Jasmine flowers are the blooms of the Asian jasmine shrub. Their strong, sweet fragrance is often used in desserts in the same manner as vanilla extract. Jasmine extract in a bottle is available at well-stocked Asian grocery stores. Jasmine water is made by floating a handful of flowers in a bowl of cold water overnight or diluting the extract with water. Use rose water or vanilla extract as a substitute.

Lemongrass* resembles a grass and has a strong lemon aroma. To use lemongrass, cut off the grassy top and root end. Peel and discard the large, tough outer leaves of the stalk until you reach the light green inner leaves. Chop it very finely for use in salads, grind it into curry pastes, or cut it into two-inch portions and bruise it to use in soup broth. Lemongrass can be found fresh in most grocery stores because it has a very long shelf life. Dried and frozen lemongrass are also available in most Asian stores.

Kaffir lime* has a thick, dark, wrinkled skin. Its glossy dark green leaves and rinds are used for a strong citrus flavor in curry pastes, soups, and salads. Kaffir limes are available in Asian grocery stores in fresh, dried, and frozen forms. Fresh kaffir lime has a slightly bitter juice that is rarely used.

La-lot leaves, also called **pepper leaves**, come from a plant in the pepper family that has shiny, heart-shaped leaves and small nuts that can be chewed like tobacco. The leaves are often used as wrappers, and when they are cooked (mostly grilled), they infuse a mild anise flavor and camphor aroma into the food. La-lot leaves can be found in well-supplied Vietnamese markets. Perilla leaves, or Japanese shiso leaves, are somewhat similar in flavor and make an exceptional substitute.

Lesser ginger* is a rhizome related to ginger but milder in flavor. The fresh form comes in tubes—long, thin, and fingerlike, with yellow meat and brown skin. It is a main ingredient for making a curry broth for Asian rice noodles. Lesser ginger is also available pickled in jars with brine.

Mustard seeds are the seeds of mustard plants or mustard greens. Mustard seeds generally come in three colors: white or yellow, brown, and black; the black seeds are the most pungent. Mustard seeds are sold whole or powdered; they are also processed into prepared mustard. White seeds are often used in European cuisines and can be found in most supermarkets. Brown and black seeds are used in Asian cuisines, especially Indian, and can be found in Indian and Asian grocery stores.

Nigella seeds*, or **black cumin seeds**, have a pungent, bitter taste and a faint sweet, fruity smell. The seeds are used mostly in curry dishes and as a garnish, such as sprinkled on top of *naan* breads. They can be found at Indian grocery stores in the spice section.

Pandan or **pandanus leaves**, also called **screw pine leaves**, are the long, slender, bladelike dark green leaves of a tropical plant. They impart a sweet floral fragrance that is popular in Southeast Asian desserts. Their intense green color is valued as a natural food coloring. Pound and grind the leaves with a little water and strain the mixture to get a liquid extract. Bottled pandan extract is available in well-stocked Asian grocery stores. Southeast Asians use pandan extract instead of vanilla extract in their cooking. Use rose or vanilla extract as a substitute.

Perilla leaves: See the entries for shiso leaves (page 12) and la-lot leaves (page 10).

Preserved turnips and **Chinese pickled radishes** are salt-cured Chinese turnips or radishes. They are used as a flavor enhancer and are salty and sweet with a crunchy texture. Chop them into small chunks before using. They are available in the dried goods section of all Asian markets.

Salam leaves are aromatic leaves from a tropical plant that grows abundantly in Indonesia and Malaysia. Fresh salam leaves are hard to find in the United States; the dried leaves are available at Asian grocery stores. Use them as you would bay leaves, which are a good substitute.

Sawtooth herb* has slender, bright, shiny green leaves with serrated edges. It emits a unique fragrance that is a combination of cilantro and mint. Sawtooth herb is served fresh to accompany many dishes; it is also included in Laotian, Thai, and Vietnamese salad dishes.

Sesame seeds* come in many varieties: black, brown, white, and yellow. The seeds are often roasted in a dry pan to enhance their pleasant nutty flavor. Sesame seeds are often used as a garnish, and their oil is often used as a flavoring agent, either by itself or mixed with another oil in stir-fries. Japanese *shojin ryori,* a type of cuisine that disdains the use of animal products and is practiced in Buddhist monasteries and temples, highlights the use of sesame seeds.

Shiso leaves (also called **Japanese shiso leaves, perilla leaves,** and **beefsteak leaves**) are heart-shaped leaves with serrated edges and are tinged with purple underneath. They are related to mint, with a faint aromatic flavor of ginger and cinnamon. They are used in salads and noodle dishes.

Star anise is a major spice in Chinese cuisine and is frequently used in other Asian cooking. These eight-pointed, star-shaped seedpods have a sweet licorice flavor. They are the products of a slender evergreen tree in the magnolia family that is native to China. They are used whole or are ground into a powder and are often added to long-simmering dishes. Star anise is one of the key elements in Chinese five-spice powder.

Sugarcane is the fresh, bamboolike stem of the sugarcane plant. Before using it, peel off the green or yellow skin and use only the yellowish white meat. It can be cut into small chunks and added to food for a sweet taste and the fresh flavor of sugarcane. Alternatively, cut it into strips to use as skewers for grilling. Peeled and canned sugarcane in brine is available in five- to eight-inch sticks.

Szechuan pepper is a hot spice that is widely used in Chinese Szechuan cuisine; it is not related to peppers or chiles. It has unique lemon-mint overtones and creates a tingly numbness in the mouth. Only the husks of Szechuan pepper are used, and they often come in a dried form. They need to be roasted and crushed before using. They also come in other forms: powder, powder mixed with salt (for Szechuan pepper salt), and powder mixed with oil (for Szechuan pepper oil).

Tamarind* is the fruit pod of a very large tamarind tree with fine, fernlike leaves. Fresh green tamarind can be used in chile dips or pickled and served as a snack. The ripe brown pulp is extracted for tamarind liquid and is used to impart a sour flavor without the tartness of lime. The tamarind liquid often is used in soups and stir-fries. At Asian grocery stores, it is available in a pulp block, powdered, or ready-made in a jar. To make tamarind liquid from the pulp, soak a one-inch cube of tamarind with one-half cup of warm water. Work the tamarind with your fingers until it disintegrates and the water turns brown and thickens. Alternatively, boil the pulp with water for five to seven minutes, or until it disintegrates. Strain the mixture through a sieve; it will make about one-third cup of tamarind liquid.

Turmeric* is a rhizome plant that is bright yellow, making it good for both coloring and flavoring. Ground turmeric is used mainly in curry powders for Indian cuisine. Fresh turmeric is hard to find; dried or ground turmeric can be substituted.

Vietnamese mint* has green and purple slender leaves with an herbaceous flavor that is cool, zippy, and spicy. This exotic herb is often added fresh to salads and soups for authentic Vietnamese, Thai, and Laotian dishes. An exact substitute is unlikely; regular mint is acceptable.

Beans, Fruits, and Vegetables

Agar is a gelatin derived from refined seaweed. It is available in many forms: a package of two rectangular ten-inch-long sticks, two- to four-ounce packages of fourteen-inch translucent strands that resemble crinkled strips of cellophane, or flakes or powder in small packages. It is widely used in Southeast Asian cooking for molded jellied sweets. To use agar sticks or strands, soak them in warm water for thirty minutes and squeeze the pieces dry. Add the agar to cold water or other cold liquid in a pot and simmer until it is completely dissolved. As a general rule, one-half stick of agar (or two-thirds of an ounce of agar strands) will thicken four cups of liquid. Ready-made dried agar sticks are also available in many sizes and colors. They need to be boiled in water or other liquid until tender and are used in iced desserts and sweet drinks.

Asian gourd, or **bottle gourd**, is a long, slender, green vegetable similar to a green zucchini. Sometimes its skin will be ripped or tough and the gourd will need to be peeled before it is cooked in a stir-fry dish or soup. Mature bottle gourds have a hard, dry shell that is water resistant and can be used as a bottle (hence the name). They are also called loofah.

Baby corn is young corn that has been harvested before maturity. It is very sweet and tender and is used in stir-fries or as a fresh vegetable to accompany chile dips. Fresh baby corn is available in well-stocked Asian produce markets, but cooked and canned baby corn are widely available. There is no comparison in taste between fresh and canned baby corn.

Bamboo shoots are the young sprouts of the bamboo bush. They have a neutral taste with a crunchy texture and absorb flavors well in various Asian dishes, especially curries. You can buy fresh, cooked, or canned bamboo shoots in Asian supermarkets. To prepare fresh bamboo shoots, trim the tips, remove the tough outer shell, and cut off the tough bottom ends. Boil the shoots with two or three changes of water, boiling each time for three to five minutes, until they are tender but still crunchy.

Banana flower, or **blossom**, is the male part at the tip of a banana flower where the female counterpart at the end develops into the banana fruit. To prepare banana flower, remove the tough red outer petals, trim back the stem, and cut the flower in half. Cook it in boiling water for five to seven minutes (this will remove any bitterness); then slice it and add it to soups or salads. The flower also can be eaten raw as an accompaniment to a main dish. It needs to be soaked in water with lime or lemon juice or rubbed with a slice of lime to keep it from turning brown.

Chana dal refers to Indian yellow split peas, or field peas, which are grown specially for drying. After they have been dried, they usually split along a natural seam. Chana dal is available both whole and split. Packages of chana dal can be found in supermarkets; chana dal is also sold in bulk in natural food stores.

Chinese broccoli has dark green leathery leaves that grow on thick stalks. The leaves, stalks, and flowers can be eaten. Peel the tough skin off the stalk before using. Regular broccoli is a good substitute.

Chinese celery is smaller than Western celery and has a stronger flavor. It is served fresh in salads or cooked in clear broth. It is used mostly in seafood dishes to counteract the fishy flavor.

Coconut is an extremely versatile plant: its leaves and trunk are used in construction; the shell of the fruit is used for fiber in the garment industry; and its fruit is used for food and in medicines. Coconut sugar, or palm sugar, is extracted from the sap of the coconut flower; palm wine, or toddy, is further refined by fermentation and distillation.

Coconut cream is the rich and creamy liquid from the first pressing of coconut milk. See Cracking and Milking Fresh Coconut, page 26.

Coconut milk is derived from processing the grated white meat of the ripe brown coconut, not to be confused with the clear coconut water (the liquid inside the fruit). The process involves steeping the freshly grated coconut meat in boiling water and letting it stand for five to ten minutes before pressing it and straining out the thick white liquid. The first pressing usually is set aside for a rich coconut cream. The second and third pressings yield a less fatty coconut milk. In markets in the United States you now can choose from many forms of coconut milk and cream: fresh from a ripe coconut, frozen, powdered, packaged in a carton, and canned. After standing on a shelf for a while, the canned coconut separates into a thick top layer of cream and a bottom layer of milk. By opening the can gently and scooping out the thick top layer, you can easily obtain coconut cream. If you shake the can before opening it, you will get coconut milk. See Cracking and Milking Fresh Coconut, page 26.

Smoked coconut is a young green coconut that has been smoked. This process intensifies the coconut's flavors, giving it a slightly smoky aroma and taste.

Young coconut is popular for its clear, refreshing water (the liquid inside the coconut), which is often served as a flavorful drink along with the tender, white coconut meat. See Cracking and Milking Fresh Coconut, page 26.

Daikon is the root of a giant white radish. It has a long, cylindrical shape resembling a white carrot. Daikon has a pleasant sweet flavor and a crunchy texture. It is often used to make Asian soup broths. In Japanese cuisine, daikon is widely used in both salads and hot dishes.

Dal, or **dhal**, is one of the principal foods of the Indian subcontinent. It is the Hindi word for any of variety of dried legumes, including peas, beans, and lentils (see "chana dal," above). Dal can also refer to an Indian dish prepared with legumes, seasonings, and spices.

Eggplant originated in India. It comes in many varieties: sizes range from a small marble to a baseball, shapes may be oval to spherical, and colors extend from white to yellow to green to purple.

Indian eggplant is pear-shaped, with a color that is similar to a standard Western eggplant but only about one-quarter of the size. Indian eggplant has a dense texture that can be cooked in stews and curries for long time without becoming mushy or disintegrating like standard eggplant.

Long eggplant, or *Asian eggplant*, is a long, green or purple fruit with a denser texture than regular purple eggplant. It often is used in salads, stir-fries, and curry dishes.

Marble eggplant grows in clusters. It is bright green and is the size of small marbles.

Thai eggplant is the size of a golf ball. It is light green with a crunchy texture. It is used as a vegetable in red or green curry and is also served raw with chile dips.

Jackfruit is a very large fruit with short, spiky, brownish green skin. Its meat is brilliant yellow or orange and has a unique, sweet flavor. Jackfruit is often used in Asian desserts because of its neutral sweetness that goes with almost anything. In the United States, jackfruit canned in syrup is readily available in Asian grocery stores.

Jicama is an underground tuber with crunchy, juicy, ivory-colored flesh and a sweet, bland flavor that suits everything from fruit cups to stir-fries. Jicama can be eaten raw or cooked after its thin, matte, sandy brown skin has been peeled.

Kabocha squash is considered a winter squash in the United States, even though it is available year-round. It has a jade green rind with celadon green streaks. When cooked, its pale orange flesh is tender, smooth, and sweet. Choose kabochas that are heavy for their size. The rind should be dull and firm; avoid any with soft spots. Kabochas are similar to pumpkins or acorn squash and are cooked the same way.

Kombu is dried giant kelp, cultivated mostly in Japan's northern seas. It is often used to make a seaweed broth called *dashi*, which is the base for all Japanese soups. Dried kombu is also commercially processed into snacks or decorative bow ties, adding flavor and interest to soups and hot pots.

Lily buds, or **lily flowers**, are the flowers of a type of day lily that have been dried. They have a unique flavor with a sweet fragrance and elastic texture. Soak lily buds in warm water to soften them before using them in soups, salads, and stir-fries.

Longan has been cultivated for centuries as a cash crop in the cool northern region of Southeast Asia. Longan fruit is round, the size of a cherry, with leathery brown skin, a very sweet flavor, and a strong, unique aroma. It can be eaten fresh and is often used as a main ingredient in Asian desserts. In the United States, imported canned longan can be found year-round. Fresh longan can be found seasonally in well-stocked Asian markets.

Long beans, also known as **yard-long beans** or **snake beans**, have slender green or purple pods that grow up to twelve inches in length. They are excellent eaten raw or cooked in stir-fried dishes. Long beans are available in most supermarkets during the spring and summer months. Green beans are a good substitute.

Lotus is a symbol of purity in most Asian cultures that relate to Buddhism. Its root is light brown, with an odd appearance similar to a chain of stiff frozen sausages. It is used as a vegetable in soups and stir-fries. Lotus seeds are available fresh for use in sweet dishes or dried for use in stews. Fresh lotus stems can be used in stir-fries and sometimes in salads.

Lychee fruit originated in China but also has been cultivated in the northern region of Southeast Asia, where it has become a local favorite. Lychee fruit is round, a little bit bigger than a cherry, with red bumpy, inedible skin and a sweet flavor that has a pleasant sour hint. In the United States, imported canned lychee is available year-round. Fresh lychee can be found seasonally in well-stocked Asian markets.

Morning glory, also called **water spinach** or **swamp cabbage**, has roughly triangular-shaped leaves and hollow stems. One variety has dark green leaves with red stalks, while the Chinese type is lighter green and has thicker stalks. The tender tips are popular for flambés or stir-fries, or they are eaten fresh as a side vegetable. Spinach is the closest substitute.

Mung beans have green skins and yellow flesh and are often used in Asian desserts. The beans are usually sold dried and prepackaged. Soak the beans in cold water for at least thirty minutes before cooking them. Drain and then boil the beans in water for five to seven minutes, or until tender.

Okra grows in pods that are ridged and tapered at the tip and contain many small seeds. Its shape and general graceful appearance gave it the alternate name of ladies' fingers. When cut open, okra pods release a gummy substance, which is one of its special characteristics. Okra originated in Africa, between West Africa and Ethiopia. It arrived in the U.S. South in the seventeenth century and became popular in Creole and Cajun cooking. Okra came to Asia in the eighteenth to nineteenth centuries. In addition to being used in cooked dishes, okra can also be dried and powdered and used as a thickening agent.

Pomelo is the giant grapefruit now readily available in almost all Asian markets in early winter. It is sweeter and less bitter than standard grapefruit and may be eaten either as a fruit or as a main ingredient in salad.

Papaya is usually eaten ripe as a fresh fruit, but unripe green papaya is very popular for the Southeast Asian green papaya salad. When choosing a fruit for green papaya salad, select one that is very hard and firm with a bright green color. Peel and seed the papaya before shredding or cutting it into fine matchstick pieces. In the United States, green papaya that is imported from Mexico is available in well-stocked Asian grocery stores.

Rambutan is a fruit with a distinctive, hairy red skin and sweet, opaque white meat. It is imported seasonally from Asia. However, canned rambutan in syrup also is readily available.

Seaweed is usually sold fresh in bulk in large, open crocks of water. It has been cleaned, trimmed, and processed, and is most commonly available in the shape of a bow tie, knot, or string. It also is sold dried in packages and is usually reconstituted before using. Seaweed can be cooked in soups and stir-fries or poached before using in salads.

Taro roots are the oval-shaped, underground tubers of taro plants. They have brown, hairy skins with encircling rings. In the United States, there are two types available: large, which is almost as big as a football, and miniature, about the size of a plum. The flesh may vary from white to cream and is often speckled with purple. Its taste is similar to a potato but with a distinctive taro flavor. Taro can be cooked and used the same way as a potato or sweet potato.

Water chestnuts add a sweet flavor, white color, and crunchy texture to many dishes, especially desserts. They are the tuber of a plant in the sedge family and are round with black skin. Fresh water chestnuts are available at well-stocked Asian markets. Choose firm, unblemished ones, and peel off the black skin before using. Canned water chestnuts are available in all supermarkets. There is no comparison between fresh and canned water chestnuts.

Yellow gram is the Indian term for whole yellow beans. The term *gram* means "chickpea," and when it is ground it becomes gram flour, also known as besan flour. Gram in other colors can be found in Indian markets, including black gram (known as *urad dal*), green gram (or mung beans), red gram (or pigeon peas), and white gram (soybeans).

Rice, Noodles, and Wrappers

Rice is the staple food of all Asian cuisines. Many varieties of rice have been cultivated according to the climates and terrains of each country in Asia. Both short- and long-grain rice are steamed and accompany almost every Asian meal.

Basmati rice is a variety of long-grain rice that is popular for its fragrance. Basmati means "the fragrant one" in Sanskrit. India and Pakistan are the largest exporters of the rice, which is available in both white and brown varieties.

Brown rice is a long-grain rice with only its inedible outer husk removed; it is not ground or polished into a smooth, white grain. The nutritious, high-fiber bran coating gives it a light tan color, nutlike flavor, and chewy texture. Brown rice is subject to rancidity, which limits its shelf life to about six months. Brown rice, or unmilled rice, now regarded as a health food, was rarely eaten in rice-staple countries, where people valued the whiteness and tenderness of the milled grains. The brown or reddish outer layers (bran) are rich in fiber and in B-group vitamins. Cook brown rice the same way as regular long-grain white rice, but add a little more water and increase the cooking time to about forty minutes.

Japanese rice, also called *Japanese pearl rice* and *sushi rice*, is a short-grain rice. The most popular sushi rice is white and very small, almost round. It contains a higher percentage of starch than other varieties. It is different from sweet, glutinous short-grain rice, which is often used in desserts, such as pounded rice *mochi*.

Jasmine rice is a long-grain rice native to Thailand; it is available almost everywhere. Before cooking, rinse the rice well with water to cleanse away any dirt and debris. Cook the rice in a pot with a tight-fitting lid using a ratio of one part rice to two parts cold water. Bring to a boil. Lower the heat, cover, and simmer for fifteen to twenty minutes, or until the water has been absorbed. Turn off the heat and let the rice stand, covered, on the still-hot stove so it can steam in the pot for ten to fifteen minutes before serving. When rice is properly cooked, it will be soft and fluffy and will have more than doubled in volume. If the rice turns out too mushy, use a little less water in the next batch. If you are using a rice cooker, follow the instructions in the manual that came with it.

Glutinous, sweet, or *sticky rice* is long-grain rice with a unique sticky quality. After it is cooked, it becomes gluey and soft and can be easily shaped into a ball. Its flavor is mild and sweet. The uncooked grains are whiter, shorter, and rounder than jasmine rice. The best way to prepare glutinous rice is to soak it for three to twelve hours in cold water, using a ratio of one part rice to three parts water. Drain the rice and then steam it over high heat in a bamboo steamer or regular steamer for fifteen to twenty minutes, or until it is tender.

Glutinous black rice is a long-grain variety of sweet or sticky rice. It has dark purple grains and a unique fragrance. It should be prepared the same way as its white counterpart, but it will take longer to cook, about twenty to thirty minutes in all. Black rice often is combined with glutinous white rice, using a ratio of one to one before soaking, to give it a desirable tender texture after it has been cooked.

Rice papers, also called **rice sheets**, are indispensable to Vietnamese food as wrappers. They are used as a light starch, and their mild flavor offsets rich, well-seasoned food. Dried, tissue-thin rice papers are made from rice flour and water and are commonly and conveniently purchased rather than made at home. Rice papers are manufactured in many sizes, from six to twelve inches in diameter; the eight-inch round is the most common. Rice papers need no further cooking, but they do require softening before use. Simply soak each whole rice paper in a bowl of warm water or brush it with warm water until it is soft and pliable.

Noodles are a Chinese creation that was adopted by all Asian cuisines, and noodle recipes have been integrated into many local signature dishes. The word *mein* in Chinese refers to noodles that are made from wheat starch, and *fun* refers to noodles made from rice and other starches, such as beans. There are many varieties of noodles, all differing in size, shape, and ingredients. In well-stocked Asian grocery stores in the United States, you can buy fresh wide or medium rice and wheat noodles and even a fresh sheet that you can slice into noodles at home. Dried noodles are readily available in all sizes and quantities. Dried noodles should be soaked or boiled in water to soften them before using. Noodles and their length symbolize longevity in most Asian cultures, so long noodles are often served for a birthday celebration meal.

Cellophane noodles, also called *glass noodles*, are made from mung bean flour. They are most often available dried in vermicelli threads. After being soaked or cooked in water, they become clear (hence the name).

Fine-thread rice noodles are thin, round noodles made from freshly ground rice flour. They are sold in small portions that resemble a bird's nest. In the United States, fresh fine-thread rice noodles are difficult to find. The closest substitute are wheat-based Japanese somen noodles (see below), which are sold in well-stocked Asian grocery stores. Cook the noodles in boiling water until soft. Drain and then rinse them with cold water before portioning into small bird's nest–sized wads.

Fine-thread wheat noodles are made from wheat flour and are often dried like vermicelli.

Medium-thread rice noodles are rice noodles that are one-quarter inch wide.

Pancit is a generic term for noodles in Filipino cuisine. Pancit noodles can be made from rice, wheat, or other ingredients.

Potato noodles are noodles made from a combination of potato flour and other flours. They come both fresh and dried and are available in many different sizes. Potato noodles lend a different taste and texture from ordinary rice and wheat noodles.

Ramen are Chinese-style wheat noodles that have become prevalent in Japan over the past century. Ramen noodles are often made into dried vermicelli and are popular as a prepackaged, quick noodle dish that can be prepared by just adding hot water.

Seaweed noodles are vermicelli noodles made from agar, a type of seaweed that naturally forms filaments.

Small rice noodles are vermicelli rice noodles.

Soba are Japanese noodles made from buckwheat flour.

Somen are Japanese noodles made from wheat flour. Instead of being cut into noodles from flattened dough, somen dough is pulled into fine strands like vermicelli and coated with vegetable oil. Various types of somen are available, each with special ingredients added, such as green tea somen and tomato somen. Somen noodles are typically served hot in winter and cold in summer, wet or dry, as either an appetizer or a meal.

Soybean noodles are small-sized noodles made from tofu (soybean curd) mixed with little wheat flour for stability. They are popular in vegetarian dishes for their high protein content.

Udon are Japanese noodles made from wheat flour. They are the same size as spaghetti but rounder in shape and softer in texture. Their taste is neutral, allowing the accompanying ingredients to shine. Udon can also be served with curry.

Wide rice noodles are one-inch-wide rice noodles.

Yellow or *egg noodles* are small yellow noodles made from flour and eggs. Fresh noodles are available in well-stocked Asian grocery stores. Dried yellow noodles are also sold prepackaged in small balls. A vegan version of yellow noodles is available made with an egg substitute. Cook the noodles in boiling water until soft.

Papadums are crispy Indian breads that are flattened into wafer-thin, round crackers, similar in shape to tortillas. They are made from lentil flour and can be unseasoned or flavored with black pepper, chile, garlic, or other seasonings. Papadums can be deep-fried, which puffs them up to almost double their original size, or roasted over an open flame, which imparts a smoky flavor. Papadums are available in Indian markets in various sizes and flavors.

Tapioca pearls are made from tapioca flour and shaped into small, medium, and large round balls. They are kneaded with lukewarm water to make a dough, or they are cooked in boiling water to make pudding.

Wrappers are another item that Asian cooking has borrowed from the Chinese for a number of dishes. Most ready-made wrappers can be cooked very quickly, helping to speed up preparation time over making wrappers from scratch. Spring roll wrappers, lumpia wrappers, and rice wrappers are made from a flour-based dough and generally come in three sizes: five-inch, nine-inch, and twelve-inch squares. They are available fresh or frozen. The larger size can be cut to the proportion needed. Wonton wrappers, about three and a half inches square, are made from flour and eggs and come in two thicknesses: very thin for deep-frying, and thick for steaming or making dumplings. Tofu sheets or skins can also be used as wrappers.

Seasonings

Candy sugar, also sold as **sugar in pieces**, is a Chinese invention made from sugarcane. It has been minimally processed to maintain the sugarcane's original flavor and fragrance. Candy sugar often comes in a plastic-wrapped stack of five-inch by one-inch blocks, with each block being one-quarter inch thick. It is light brown and similar in color to brown sugar. It's quite brittle and melts easily when heated. Break or chop the sugar into small chunks and use it to make syrup or add a flavorful sweetness to food. Brown sugar is an excellent substitute.

Chile sauces are prepared Asian seasonings that can be used as condiments or mixed into a dish.

Asian black bean garlic sauce is a sweet, mild, and smoky chile sauce that often is used as a flavor enhancer in salad dressings and soups.

Chile paste with soybean oil is a sweet, mild, and smoky chile sauce that often is used as a flavor enhancer in salad dressings and soups. It is commonly used in Southeast Asian cuisine, especially Thai cuisine.

Chinese white plum sauce is a mild, sweet-and-sour syrup. It is used as a sauce for delicately flavored dishes, such as Chinese crêpes and corn fritters.

Ichimi and *shichimi togarashi* are chile-based condiments that add heat to Japanese dishes. They are comprised of dried red chiles, sesame seeds, sea vegetables, orange zest, and ginger. They are usually sold in small bottles containing about half an ounce.

Sambal oelek is hot-and-sour condiment made from ground red chiles in a vinegar mixture. It is popular for adding a chile zest to a bowl of soup and to various sauces.

Sriracha sauce is a hot, sweet-and-sour sauce that can add spicy heat to any dish.

Sweet chile sauce is a sweet-and-sour sauce with evidence of mild red chile chunks. It is a product of Thailand and is a popular sauce for fried or barbecued dishes.

Vietnamese garlic-and-chile sauce adds heat to many Vietnamese dishes and sauces and is also used as a condiment.

Curry paste comes in many varieties. It is available in small cans for one-time use and in big plastic tubs for several uses. It should always be refrigerated after opening. Ready-made curry paste is convenient and saves time, but some contain animal products (such as shrimp paste) and preservatives. To all food connoisseurs, a fresh curry paste made from scratch using a mortar with pestle is worth the extra effort.

Hoisin sauce is a Chinese savory sauce that is a mainstay on Chinese and Vietnamese dining tables. It is used as a condiment for soups and snacks and as a seasoning for sauces and many dishes. It consists of fermented soybeans, vinegar, garlic, chiles, herbs, and spices. Hoisin sauce adds sweet, savory, and a little spicy flavor to any dish.

Maggi Seasoning Sauce is a brand-name multipurpose seasoning that originated in Switzerland but is now popular throughout Asia. It serves as a secret flavor enhancer in most marinade recipes. A few drops can improve flavor dramatically. A similar product under the brand name of Golden Mountain Thai Seasoning Sauce also is available.

Mirin is Japanese rice wine made from sweet glutinous rice and koji, a yeastlike culture. It is sweeter than sake (rice wine) and is used as a cooking wine in Japanese cuisine. It comes in two versions: real mirin, also known as *hon mirin*, with a pleasing flavor and high alcohol content of 14 percent, and *mirin-fuhmi*, or mirin flavoring, with a cheap imitation flavor and only 1 percent alcohol content.

Palm sugar and **coconut sugar** are made from the nectar of palm or coconut flowers respectively. They have a distinctive flavor and fragrance and a pale, light brown color. In the United States, palm sugar is sold as a paste in plastic bottles or as crystallized discs in clear plastic wrap in most well-stocked Asian grocery stores. Chop or grate either sugar into small chunks or heat it in a microwave for one to two minutes until melted so you can measure it before using. Store it the same way as ordinary sugar.

Rock sugar, also called **crystal sugar**, originated in China and is shaped like small rocks. It is made from either sugarcane and/or sugar beets and is light brown or clear and has the fragrance of the ingredient used to make it. Rock sugar melts readily when heated. Break it into small pieces with a kitchen mallet or the back of a knife, and use it to make syrup or add it to food to obtain sweetness with flavor.

Shaoxing rice wine, also known as **yellow wine**, is Chinese cooking wine made from fermented rice. The most popular one comes from Shaoxing (considered the Napa Valley of Asia), in the Zhejiang Province. It has a rich flavor with a relatively low alcohol content. It is widely available at Asian grocery stores. Sherry and other sweet cooking wines are good substitutes.

Stir-fry sauce, or **vegetarian oyster sauce**, is similar to oyster sauce but is made from plant-based ingredients, such as mushrooms, sea vegetables, and sweetened soy sauce. It is used mostly in stir-fried vegetable dishes. Stir-fry sauce comes in many varieties: mushroom stir-fry sauce, vegetarian stir-fry sauce, and vegetarian marinade. It must be refrigerated after opening and should keep for about six months.

Vegetable base and **bouillon** are flavor enhancers made by reducing vegetable stock into a paste or powder. They add saltiness and an intense vegetable flavor. They are used sparingly to improve the taste of a dish without using MSG.

Cracking and Milking Fresh Coconut

Young Coconuts   Young coconuts are prized for their tender meat and fresh, tasty juice. If possible, choose a young coconut that has a green outer skin. In most Asian markets, the green skin has been removed and only the white husk, in the shape of an upside-down cone, remains.

Lay the young coconut on its side. Using a cleaver or a large, sturdy chef's knife, chop off the top (pointed) cone section of the coconut in one piece and pour out the clear juice. Using a long-handled spoon, scrape out the tender, white meat through the opening. Do not scrape too hard or too close to the shell; otherwise, the brown inner shell will mar the color of the white coconut meat. The clear juice can be served as a beverage and the white meat as a fruit. Both the juice and meat are often used to sweeten and flavor cooked dishes.

Mature Coconuts   For coconut cream and milk, choose a very heavy mature coconut with brown skin and husk. In most Asian markets, a mature coconut will come already husked and peeled and left in its hard shell. To open the coconut, use the back of a cleaver or a hammer to strike a blow right in the middle of the coconut to crack it, preferably in half. Use the blade of the cleaver or a flat-tipped screwdriver to pry the crack open and drain out the clear liquid. Score the white coconut meat that is still attached to the shell into small sections. With the sturdy tip of a blade or screwdriver, pry and yank the white meat off the shell.

To obtain only the white meat for cooking applications, use a vegetable peeler and peel off the thin brown skin underneath the white meat. Chop the white meat into fine chunks or grate it into fine strips with a grater, such as a box grater. Use the freshly grated coconut immediately, or store it in an air-tight container in the refrigerator for up to twenty-four hours.

To obtain coconut cream and milk, leave the brown skin underneath the meat intact. Grate or process the meat into fine flakes in a food processor. Transfer the flaked coconut to a heatproof bowl and cover it with boiling water. Let it stand until the mixture is cool enough to be easily handled. With both hands, knead and squeeze the mixture for two to three minutes, until a thick cream is released. Place a fine sieve over a bowl; scoop a handful of the mixture into it and squeeze out the cream. Alternatively, use cheesecloth in place of a sieve. Continue the process until all of the coconut has been squeezed.

Reserve this first pressing for rich coconut cream that will be used in desserts and marinades. For a lighter version to be used as coconut milk, cover the coconut again with boiling water and repeat the squeezing process. This can be done two or three times, with each time producing a lighter milk.

Special Equipment

Clay Pot or Chinese Clay Pot

This simple and inexpensive cooking utensil has its origins in China and is used throughout Asia. It is a cooking and serving tool in one, as food can be cooked and served directly from the clay pot. It is handmade, with a natural clay color, and is partially glazed on the inside. It usually comes with one large handle or two small handles and a tight-fitting lid.

There are many types of Chinese clay pots, each with different qualities, but most are intended for short-term use. Some of the clay pots are secured with wire to ensure that even if a pot happens to crack during cooking the food will still hold together and be completely cooked during this final use of the pot. A clay pot with a flat bottom is intended for use on top of the stove, but it can go into an oven for the purpose of keeping food warm or reheating it. When using a clay pot on a stove with an open flame, the fine clay of the pot will lightly filter a smoky flavor into the food.

When cooking with a clay pot, start with a low heat to warm the pot, and then adjust the heat to the desired temperature. Rapid heating will cause the pot to crack, as the clay can't expand fast enough on high heat. Clay pots are available in many sizes at Chinese and

Asian grocery stores. A regular metal pot with a tight-fitting lid is a good substitute.

Mortar with Pestle

There are two types of mortars (bowls), each serving a particular purpose: a stone mortar and a clay mortar. The stone mortar and pestle are made of solid granite or sandstone and are hand carved from a selected piece of the stone by artisans. The mortar is very heavy and sturdy and has a stubby shape; its mouth is wide and has a very thick rim. It's perfect for the heavy pounding required for making chile and curry pastes. An exception is the Indonesian mortar with pestle, as it is made from lava rock. The mortar is formed into a flat container, and the pestle is designed not for pounding but for rolling back and forth to crush ingredients on top of the mortar.

A clay mortar is easy to make by hand. The mortar is made of clay and is kiln fired, and its pestle is carved out of wood. It is a lot less expensive than the stone mortar, but it has a shorter life and is disposable. It is shaped like a tall cylinder, with a wide mouth and narrow base. It is light, unstable, and not suitable for making pastes. Its main function is to serve as a mixing or tossing bowl, as it can only withstand minimal grinding. The famous Green Papaya Salad (page 100) calls for this kind of mortar for mixing and tossing its ingredients.

Shredder and Slicer

Shredders and slicers are essential for any kitchen, especially a vegetarian kitchen, so cooks can easily cut various kinds of vegetables into assorted shapes and sizes. You can choose from hand shredders, box graters, box slicers, mandolines, and other shredding devices with blades that can produce slices of various widths and shapes. A shredder not only helps reduce the preparation time involved with cutting fruits and vegetables but it also cuts them more thinly and uniformly than is possible to do by hand.

Steamer

Many types of Chinese steamers are typical in Asian cooking. A multilayer steamer made of metal and bamboo (a type of steamer used for *dim sum*) in various sizes is an essential tool in every Asian kitchen. A wok with a tight-fitting lid can also be used as a steamer by adding crisscross bars to hold a plate of food over boiling water.

Thai and Laotian people invented a cylindrical bamboo steamer to cook sweet, sticky, long-grain rice (the type of rice that is used in the dessert Sticky Rice and Mangoes, page 31), which is called by various names in the United States: sweet rice, sticky rice, or glutinous rice. A bamboo steamer set comes with a bamboo cylinder and a narrow-necked pot for boiling water. The bamboo cylinder is handwoven from dried bamboo strips into a cone shape, about ten inches in diameter at the opening and about twelve inches tall. The cylinder sits snugly on the narrow-necked pot of boiling water. Any kind of lid that fits in the cylinder can be used to trap the steam. A regular steamer can also be used with a little adjustment: just line its steam tray with cheesecloth so the rice grains won't fall through the steaming holes.

Wok

Asian people borrowed the wok and stir-fry cooking techniques from the Chinese, and now the wok has become indispensable in all Asian kitchens. This thin metal bowl with a handle serves many purposes: stir-frying, deep-frying, steaming, boiling, smoking, and more. Traditionally it is made of rolled steel, which provides excellent heat control, but it also can be made of sheet iron, anodized aluminum, or stainless steel. It comes in various sizes—from small, with one long handle for tossing the food, to large, with two handles to deal with a large volume of food. The advantage of stir-frying in a wok, especially mixtures that include a lot of vegetables, lies in the speed, which consequently minimizes the loss of vitamins, color, and flavor in fresh food. A flat-bottomed wok has been introduced for use on an electric, flat-topped stove in the Western kitchen. Season the wok after each use so it won't rust. Clean and dry the wok thoroughly, and then heat it and rub it with a little vegetable oil.

Indian Baked Spiced-Bread Dessert
(Shahi Tukda), p. 54

Indian Lentil-and-Spinach Dal
(Palak Dal), p. 58

Burma

Curried Noodles
Mohingha

Serves 6

This popular curry dish is considered a soup in its native land and can be conveniently found at almost every hawker food stand. It can be eaten any time of day, although Burmese prefer it at the crack of dawn. Neighborhood vendors who specialize in this dish make their fortune providing this local favorite and fiercely guard their secret formula.

This recipe combines ingredients from the best of two Asian cuisines—curry from India and noodles from China. For home cooks, a little tweak with the amount of ingredients in the spice paste will personalize the dish as your own. Simple cooking techniques are required to make the three separate components: curry, noodles, and accompaniments. Just before serving, combine all three together in your favorite proportions.

To make the spice paste, combine all the ingredients in a food processor. Process into a smooth paste, adding a small amount of water as needed to facilitate blending.

To make the curry broth, heat the oil in a saucepan over medium heat. Stir in the prepared spice paste and cook and stir for 3 to 4 minutes, until light brown and fragrant.

Add the vegetable stock, coconut milk, lemongrass, and bamboo shoots. Bring to a boil, decrease the heat, and simmer for 3 to 5 minutes. Add the tofu, soy sauce, sugar, vegetable base, and salt. Simmer for 5 minutes.

Stir in the chickpea-flour mixture. Cook and stir for 1 to 2 minutes, until the broth begins to thicken. Remove from the heat. Stir in the lemon juice. Adjust the seasonings to taste. Keep hot until ready to serve.

Spice Paste

$1^1/_2$ cups chopped yellow onions

$^1/_4$ cup chopped lemongrass, tender midsection only

3 tablespoons peeled and chopped fresh ginger

3 tablespoons chopped garlic

2 tablespoons chopped fresh red chiles, more or less to taste

1 tablespoon fermented bean curds (optional)

1 teaspoon ground turmeric

Curry Broth

3 tablespoons vegetable oil

3 cups vegetable stock

3 cups coconut milk

2 to 3 stalks lemongrass, tender midsection only, cut into 2-inch strips and smashed to lightly open

$1^1/_2$ cups thinly sliced fresh or canned bamboo shoots

1 pound firm tofu, diced

2 tablespoons light soy sauce

1 tablespoon sugar, or more to taste

1 tablespoon vegetable base (flavor enhancer or bouillon cube)

$^1/_2$ teaspoon salt

2 tablespoons chickpea flour or cornstarch mixed with $^1/_4$ cup water

3 tablespoons freshly squeezed lemon or lime juice, or more to taste

To prepare the accompaniments, heat the oil in a small pan over medium heat. Add the shallots and cook and stir for 3 to 5 minutes, until light brown, fragrant, and crispy, taking care that they do not burn. Drain on absorbent paper. Arrange the shallots, sliced onion, cilantro leaves, and lemon wedges on a platter.

To cook the noodles, bring a large pot of water to a full boil. Stir in the noodles and cook until tender (1 to 2 minutes for fresh noodles or 4 to 5 minutes for dried noodles). Drain and rinse with warm water. Distribute among 6 serving bowls.

To serve, ladle the hot curry broth over the noodles. Serve immediately. Pass the accompaniments at the table.

Accompaniments

¼ cup vegetable oil
½ cup thinly sliced shallots
1 cup thinly sliced white onion
1 cup fresh cilantro leaves
1 whole lemon or lime, cut into 6 wedges

Noodles

8 to 10 ounces fresh vermicelli noodles (any kind) or yellow noodles, or 4 to 5 ounces dried noodles

Dried Sour Curry
Kyet Thar Hin

Serves 6

With Burma's close proximity to India, Burmese foods have taken on the basics of Indian curry but have been personalized with native ingredients, such as lemongrass, kaffir lime, and local fermented delicacies. By using a touch of lime juice, the Burmese make this dish sour and clearly distinguishable from traditional Indian curry. Most Asian curries contain a high proportion of flavored liquid to encourage eating more starch; some have so much liquid they are even considered soups. This slow-cooked dish, however, allows more time for the curry to become drier, with condensed flavors that seep through its ingredients. Serve it with steamed rice.

3 tablespoons vegetable oil

1 teaspoon sesame oil

2 cups chopped yellow onions

3 tablespoons minced garlic

2 tablespoons minced fresh cilantro roots or stems

1 tablespoon minced red chiles, more or less to taste

1 tablespoon ground coriander

1 teaspoon ground turmeric

2 cinnamon sticks

3 to 4 whole fresh kaffir lime leaves, dried kaffir lime leaves, or bay leaves

3 to 4 cloves

2 cups diced firm or fried tofu

2 cups peeled and diced taro or potatoes

2 cups thinly sliced button mushrooms

1 1/2 cups chopped tomatoes, or 6 to 8 ounces canned chopped tomatoes

1 stalk lemongrass, tender midsection only, cut into several 2-inch strips and smashed to lightly open

3 tablespoons fermented bean curds (optional)

2 tablespoons light soy sauce

2 tablespoons sugar, or more to taste

1 tablespoon vegetable base (flavor enhancer or bouillon cube)

Salt, to taste

1/2 cup freshly squeezed lime juice

1/2 cup julienned colorful bell peppers, for garnish

3 to 4 sprigs cilantro, for garnish

1 lime, cut into 6 wedges

Combine the vegetable oil and sesame oil in a pot over medium heat. Add the onions and cook and stir for 4 to 5 minutes, until light brown and fragrant. Stir in the garlic, cilantro roots or stems, chiles, coriander, turmeric, cinnamon, kaffir lime leaves, and cloves. Cook and stir for 2 to 3 minutes.

Stir in the tofu, taro, mushrooms, tomatoes, lemongrass, optional fermented bean curds, soy sauce, sugar, vegetable base, and salt to taste. Decrease the heat to low, partially cover with a lid, and simmer for 15 to 20 minutes, until the vegetables are done and the sauce thickens. Check occasionally and add a little water if the mixture seems dry or starts to stick or burn on the bottom.

Stir in the lime juice. Adjust the seasonings to taste. Transfer to a serving platter and garnish with the bell peppers and cilantro sprigs. Serve the dish with the lime wedges on the side.

Nutty Snacks
Ghin Thoke

Serves 6

In Western countries, ready-mixed nuts in a can serve as an easy snack at a cocktail party or a prelude to a meal. Burmese serve a similar dish with hot tea during the pastime of conversation, similar to English biscuits at teatime, or even as a nibble at a round table while sharing a bottle of whisky or beer. Locals consider this dish a salad, mixing in more pickled ingredients, such as Burmese pickled tea leaves (laphet), garlic, ginger, and so forth, and then adding lime juice. Even more conveniently, we can just incorporate the ready-mixed nuts into the recipe and enjoy this nutty, salty, and sour snack.

¼ cup vegetable oil

1 tablespoon sesame oil

¼ cup very thinly sliced shallots

¼ cup very thinly sliced garlic

1 cup fried yellow split peas or split chana dal, or mixed nuts and seeds of your choice

1 cup roasted peanuts

1 cup roasted cashew nuts

1 cup roasted or fried nuts and beans (such as fava beans) of your choice

3 tablespoons roasted black and white sesame seeds or other roasted seeds

½ cup pickled ginger or Japanese sushi ginger, sliced into matchsticks

2 red jalape–o or serrano chiles, seeded and thinly sliced into fine matchsticks

2 tablespoons freshly squeezed lime juice, or more to taste

Salt, to taste

Heat the vegetable oil and sesame oil in a small pan over medium heat. Add the shallots and cook and stir for 3 to 5 minutes, until light brown, fragrant, and crispy, taking care that they do not burn. Drain on absorbent paper. In the same pan, add the garlic and cook and stir for 3 to 5 minutes, until light brown, fragrant, and crispy. Remove the garlic from the pan and set aside.

Combine the fried split peas, roasted peanuts, roasted cashew nuts, roasted or fried nuts, and roasted seeds in the pan with the oil left over from the shallots and garlic. Place over medium-high heat and cook and stir for 2 to 3 minutes. Remove from the heat and let cool to lukewarm.

Just before serving, combine the nut mixture with the shallots, garlic, pickled ginger, chiles, lime juice, and salt to taste. Toss until well combined. Transfer to a serving platter. Serve warm or at room temperature.

Rice
Ohn Htamin

Serves 6

Every Asian country along the equator cultivates coconut trees successfully and produces coconut products abundantly. With rice as a staple for most Asian people, coconut rice dishes have been created with a local touch that represents the country and its cuisine. Burmese have their own as well and serve this simple coconut rice with their curries and other intensely flavored dishes. Garnishes of crunchy fried shallots and coconut flakes provide a contrast in texture to the soft, creamy rice.

3 tablespoons vegetable oil

1/4 cup thinly sliced shallots

3 cups jasmine rice or long-grain white rice, rinsed with cold water and drained

1 3/4 cups (one 14-ounce can) coconut milk or cream

1 3/4 cups (one 14-ounce can) vegetable stock or water

1 tablespoon vegetable base (flavor enhancer or bouillon cube)

1 tablespoon sugar

1/2 teaspoon salt

2 tablespoons coconut flakes, roasted in a dry pan until light brown, for garnish

Heat the oil in a medium pot over medium heat. Add the shallots and cook and stir for 3 to 5 minutes, until light brown, fragrant, and crispy, taking care that they do not burn. Drain on absorbent paper. Set aside for garnish.

Add the rice, coconut milk, vegetable stock, vegetable base, sugar, and salt to the oil remaining in the pot. Stir to mix well. Bring to a boil over medium-high heat. Decrease the heat to low and cover the pot with a lid. Cook for 18 to 20 minutes, or until the rice is tender and all the liquid has been absorbed. Check the rice occasionally to make sure it is not burning on the bottom of the pot.

Fluff the rice with a fork, and then transfer it to a serving platter. Garnish with the reserved shallots and the coconut flakes.

Split-Pea Cakes

Be Ya Kiaw

Makes 24 cakes; serves 6

This dish is popular as a savory snack for an afternoon tea and is sometimes served as a side dish to a curry meal. It incorporates many Indian influences, but the addition of spicy chiles is a Burmese invention. This recipe is easy to make, and the finished product keeps well in the freezer. There are two methods for preparing the split peas in this recipe: you can either soak them overnight until they are saturated with water and swollen, or you can boil the un-soaked beans until they are tender.

1 cup dried yellow split peas

1 1/2 cups chopped yellow onions

1/2 cup chopped fresh cilantro

1 tablespoon minced Thai or jalape-o chiles, more or less to taste

1 tablespoon light soy sauce

1 tablespoon sugar

1 tablespoon vegetable base (flavor enhancer or bouillon cube)

1/2 teaspoon ground turmeric

1/2 teaspoon salt

3 cups vegetable oil, for frying

1 small white onion, peeled, cut in half, and thinly sliced

1/4 cup chopped fresh cilantro leaves, for garnish

1 lemon or lime, cut into 6 wedges

Soak the split peas in water to cover for 8 to 12 hours. Drain.

If you do not soak the split peas, you will need to boil them. Cover the split peas with plenty of water. Bring to a boil and cook just until the peas are tender enough to be mashed between your fingers. (Do not cook them until they break apart; they should still retain their shape.) Rinse the split peas with cold water. Drain thoroughly.

Transfer the soaked or cooked split peas to a food processor. Add the yellow onions, cilantro, chiles, soy sauce, sugar, vegetable base, turmeric, and salt. Process until smooth and well combined. Be careful not to overprocess or the mixture will separate.

With damp hands, mold about 2 tablespoons of the mixture into a patty, about 2 inches in diameter and 1/3 inch thick. Repeat the process to make additional patties.

Heat the oil in a wok or deep pan to 375 degrees F. The oil should have a depth of at least 2 inches. Gently drop the patties into the hot oil to fit loosely in the wok. Fry, turning occasionally, for 4 to 5 minutes, or until golden brown all over. Transfer the fried cakes to a rack or absorbent paper to drain the oil.

To serve, arrange the cakes on a serving platter. Sprinkle with the white onion and cilantro leaves. Pass the lemon wedges at the table so diners can squeeze the juice over the cakes just before eating.

Tofu Dry Curry
Wetha See Byan

Serves 6

This popular Burmese dish showcases a local style, resulting in a curry that is drier than traditional Indian curries. For this dish to be successful, the ingredients need to be cooked long enough to release their maximum flavors and reach their full potential. Some chefs "cook" with their noses, and curry chefs constantly sniff the air to ensure a mature curry aroma before proceeding with the next cooking steps. Serve this curry with steamed rice.

Combine the onions, garlic, ginger, chile, optional chile flakes, and turmeric in a food processor or blender. Pulse until thoroughly combined.

Heat the oil in a medium pot over medium-low heat. Add the onion mixture and cook, stirring occasionally, for 8 to 10 minutes, until fragrant and almost dry. Add a little water if the mixture sticks or burns on the bottom of the pot.

Increase the heat to medium-high and add the tofu, mushrooms, tamarind liquid, lemongrass, soy sauce, sugar, and vegetable base. Cook and stir for 5 to 6 minutes, until all the liquid has been absorbed, adding a small amount of water, if necessary, to avoid scorching. Adjust the seasonings to taste.

Remove from the heat and stir in the bell pepper and cilantro leaves.

2 cups chopped yellow onions

3 tablespoons chopped garlic

2 tablespoons peeled and chopped fresh ginger

2 tablespoons chopped red chile, more or less to taste

1 teaspoon dried red chile flakes (optional)

1 teaspoon ground turmeric

3 tablespoons vegetable oil

1 pound fried or pressed tofu, diced

1/4 pound dried black mushrooms, soaked in warm water to soften and then drained

1/3 cup tamarind liquid

1/4 cup very thinly sliced lemongrass, tender midsection only

3 tablespoons light soy sauce

2 tablespoons sugar, or more to taste

1 tablespoon vegetable base (flavor enhancer or bouillon cube)

1 cup julienned red bell pepper

1/2 cup whole fresh cilantro leaves

Asian Fusion

China

Almond Cake in Ginger Sauce
Gueng Ja Hang Yan Je Lei

Serves 6

In the old days, cold desserts were a rare and special treat in Asia. Thanks to refrigeration, jelled desserts, ice cream, and frosty sweets are easily found indulgences nowadays. The Chinese have many kinds of jellied dessert cakes, and almonds are the most popular ingredient in them. Instead of almonds, other nuts and fruits, such as mangoes, pineapple, or strawberries, can be substituted.

To make the cake, soak the almonds in the water for 3 to 6 hours, until they are fully expanded.

Combine the almonds, their soaking liquid, and the almond extract in a food processor or blender. Process until smooth.

Pour the almond mixture into a pot. Add the sugar and agar powder. Bring to a boil over medium heat. Decrease the heat and simmer for 2 to 3 minutes, or until the agar and sugar are dissolved. Remove from the heat and stir in the coconut milk. Pour into a shallow tray and refrigerate for 1 to 2 hours, or until firm.

To make the sauce, combine the water, sugar, and ginger in a medium pot over medium heat. Bring to a boil. Decrease the heat to medium-low, cover partially with a lid, and simmer for 25 to 30 minutes, until the mixture turns into a thin golden syrup. Strain through a fine sieve and discard the solids.

To serve, cut the cake into thin slices and distribute among serving bowls. Ladle the sauce over the cake to barely cover the slices. Sprinkle with additional brown sugar. Serve at room temperature.

Almond Cake

1/2 cup chopped raw almonds
4 cups water
1 teaspoon almond extract
1 cup sugar
2 ounces agar powder
1/2 cup coconut milk

Ginger Sauce

4 cups water
1/3 cup brown sugar, plus more for garnish
1/4 cup peeled and coarsely chopped fresh ginger

Braised Pears in Sweet Wine
Mat Jin Syut Li

Serves 6

Chinese culture includes a lot of symbolism, and fruits and vegetables have significant meanings beyond their delicious tastes and flavors. For example, pomegranates signify fertility because of their many seeds, peaches indicate longevity because of the tree's long life, and mandarin oranges, whose name in Chinese sounds like the word for gold, connote prosperity. The word fen li in Chinese means "divorce," which sounds uncomfortably close to li, the word for "pear." For this reason, pears are often served whole and should never be shared among spouses, lovers, or close friends. This dessert makes one pear per serving and is too delicious to share.

6 large, firm, ripe pears (preferably Anjou or Chinese sweet pears), with long stems intact

1 to 1½ cups sweet white wine or dessert wine (such as Muscat or Chinese sweet wine)

1 (1-inch) piece peeled and thinly sliced fresh ginger, more or less to taste (optional)

1 tablespoon sugar, or more to taste

1 tablespoon honey, or more to taste

Salt, to taste

Gently peel all of the skin from the pears. Put the pears in a deep pot that's just large enough for them to fit snugly. Pour in the wine. Add the ginger and some water or additional wine, if necessary, to cover the pears three-quarters of the way up.

Bring to a boil over medium-high heat. Decrease the heat, partially cover the pot with a lid, and simmer for 30 minutes, occasionally dousing the pears with the hot liquid. Remove the pears from the liquid and set them aside.

Bring the remaining liquid to a boil and add the sugar and honey. Boil for 5 to 6 minutes, until the liquid turns into a thin syrup. Taste and add more sugar or honey if it is not sweet enough.

To serve warm, place each still-warm pear in small, individual serving bowls, and pour the warm syrup over the pears. To serve cold, chill the pears and syrup in the refrigerator and serve in small, individual bowls.

Cold Sing Dou Noodles
Sing Dou Ma Laat Min

Serves 6

During the cold months in China, hot food is served. During the warm months, when some parts of China are exceptionally hot, cold noodles are very appropriate. This dish can be prepared well in advance and set aside to serve at room temperature or refrigerated to serve at a later time. The recipe is simple, and additional cooked or fresh vegetables of your choice can be added.

For the noodles, bring a large pot of water to a boil. Add the noodles and cook, stirring occasionally, until tender (1 to 2 minutes for fresh noodles or 4 to 5 minutes for dried noodles). Drain in a colander. Rinse with cold water and drain again. Set aside.

For the vegetables, bring another pot of water to a boil. Add the bean sprouts and carrot ribbons and blanch for 30 to 45 seconds. Drain in a colander. Rinse with cold water and drain again. Set aside.

To make the sesame sauce, combine all the ingredients in a bowl. Beat gently with a spoon or whisk to mix well.

To serve, combine the cooked noodles with the bean sprouts, carrot ribbons, and sesame seeds in a mixing bowl. Add the sesame sauce and toss gently to mix well. Transfer to a serving platter and sprinkle with the pepper and green onion.

Noodles and Vegetables

8 to 10 ounces fresh thin wheat noodles, or 4 to 5 ounces dried thin wheat noodles

1/3 pound (about 3 cups) bean sprouts

1 carrot peeled and shaved with a vegetable peeler into short, thin ribbons (about 1 cup)

1 tablespoon roasted black and white sesame seeds

1/2 teaspoon ground white pepper, for garnish

2 tablespoons thinly sliced green onion, both green and white parts, for garnish

Sesame Sauce

Makes about 2/3 cup

1/4 cup sesame paste (tahini) or roasted sesame seeds ground into a paste

1 tablespoon sesame oil

1 tablespoon Chinese chile oil, or more to taste

1 tablespoon sweet soy sauce

1 tablespoon light soy sauce or seasoning soy sauce (such as Maggi Seasoning Sauce or mushroom-flavored soy sauce)

1 tablespoon sugar, or more to taste

1 tablespoon Chinese black rice vinegar or rice vinegar

Fried Rice with Vegetable Fu Yang
Fu Yang

Serves 6

Fried rice originated in China. The Chinese also invented the wok stir-fry cooking method. These influences were absorbed throughout Asia, and local versions of fried rice, such as Thai khao pad *and Indonesian* nasi goreng, *gained popularity. Leftover cold rice is typically used; it is preferred for its dry texture, which absorbs seasonings very well. Vegetables of your choice can be used. Just take into account their cooking time, and cut them into uniform thin slices so they cook evenly and all are done at the same time.*

Heat the oil in a wok over high heat. Add the garlic and cook and stir for 1 to 2 minutes, until light brown and fragrant. Add the onion, green beans, bell peppers, and water chestnuts and cook and stir for 2 to 3 minutes.

Stir in the rice and mix all the ingredients thoroughly. Sprinkle with the sugar, soy sauce, stir-fry sauce, vegetable base, and sesame oil. Cook and stir for 2 to 3 minutes, until well combined and heated through.

Add the optional bean sprouts and the green onions. Cook and stir for 1 to 2 minutes longer. Adjust the seasonings to taste.

Transfer to a serving platter. Sprinkle with the pepper.

3 tablespoons vegetable oil

3 tablespoons minced garlic

1 cup thinly sliced yellow onion

1 cup thinly sliced green beans or snow peas

1 cup julienned bell peppers (red, orange, and/or yellow)

1 cup peeled and julienned water chestnuts or jicama

3 cups cooked or steamed rice (prepared from 1½ cups uncooked rice), or 3 cups chilled leftover rice, crumbled

3 tablespoons sugar, or more to taste

2 tablespoons light soy sauce

2 tablespoons vegetarian stir-fry sauce

1 tablespoon vegetable base (flavor enhancer or bouillon)

1 teaspoon sesame oil

2 cups bean sprouts (optional)

¼ cup thinly sliced green onions, both green and white parts

1 teaspoon ground pepper, for garnish

Chinese Crêpes
Chung Sik Yut Namm Cheun Gyun

Makes 18 to 20 crêpes; serves 6

Occasionally, eating rice and grains can become mundane, so a variety of wrappers were created to give the starch part of the meal a different taste, texture, and appearance. For lack of a better word, I call these soft wrappers "crêpes," even though this term is not characteristic of Chinese cuisine. Freshly made wrappers are easy to prepare, and ready-made wrappers are also widely available in the refrigerated or freezer section of most supermarkets. For more fun, line up all elements of this dish—wrappers, filling, and condiments—and let your guests assemble their own.

Crêpes (use the following recipe or use 18 to 20 ready-made soft wrappers)

1 1/2 cups all-purpose flour or a combination of all-purpose flour and rice flour

1/4 cup cornstarch

1 1/2 cups vegetable stock, plus more as needed

2 tablespoons vegetable oil, plus more for frying the crêpes

2 teaspoons sesame oil

To make the crêpes, put all the ingredients in a mixing bowl. Stir until well combined. Add more vegetable stock or a little water, as needed, to make a thin, runny batter.

To cook each crêpe, heat a 6-inch nonstick pan over medium heat. Brush the pan's surface with a thin coat of oil. Stir the batter and ladle about 1/4 cup into the pan. Tilt the pan and swirl the batter to thinly coat the pan's surface. Cook the crêpe 1 to 2 minutes on each side, until it is firm, dry, and light brown, turning it once with a flat spatula. Repeat the process until the batter is used up. Stack the crêpes on a serving plate.

Prepare the filling just before serving. Heat the oil in a wok over high heat. Stir in the garlic and ginger. Cook for 1 to 2 minutes, until light brown and fragrant. Add the remaining ingredients and stir to mix well. Cook for 3 to 4 minutes, until the vegetables are tender to your liking. The mixture should be fairly dry.

For self-service, spread about ¼ teaspoon of the plum sauce and/or hoisin sauce per wrapper and top with a portion of the filling. Wrap the crêpe over the filling and roll into a log. Top with the hot mustard to taste.

Filling

3 tablespoons vegetable oil

2 tablespoons minced garlic

2 tablespoons peeled and minced fresh ginger

2 cups chopped firm tofu

1 cup matchstick-sliced snow peas or cabbage

1 cup matchstick-sliced carrot

1 cup thinly sliced mushrooms of your choice

½ cup thinly sliced yellow onion

2 tablespoons Shaoxing rice wine or sherry

2 tablespoons sugar

1 tablespoon soy sauce or soy paste

1 tablespoon vegetarian stir-fry sauce

1 teaspoon sesame oil

1 teaspoon ground pepper

Condiments

1 bottle Chinese sweet plum sauce

1 bottle hoisin sauce

¼ cup Chinese hot mustard, or powdered mustard mixed with water (using a 1:1 ratio)

Hot-and-Sour Soup
Sayun Laat Tong

Serves 6

Most Chinese soups are a clear, plain broth, similar to consommé. Hot-and-sour soups are mainly featured in Southeast Asian cuisine, such as Thai and Vietnamese. There is always an exception to the rule, though, and this soup is a special one in Chinese cooking. The sour taste comes from rice vinegar and the heat comes from ground white pepper. Chinese white pepper can be surprisingly very hot; too much can be overwhelming and can make a dish inedible.

If using dried mushrooms, soak them in warm water for 15 minutes. Drain and squeeze out the excess water. Slice the mushrooms into thin strips about the same size as the bamboo shoots and carrot.

Bring the vegetable stock to a boil in a pot over medium heat. Add the mushrooms, bamboo shoots, carrot, and onion and cook for 2 to 3 minutes. Add the wine, vinegar, soy sauce, vegetable base, pepper, and salt and bring to a boil. Decrease the heat, cover with a lid, and simmer for 4 to 5 minutes.

Add the tofu and optional soymilk. Cook uncovered for 2 minutes longer. Taste and add more soy sauce, vinegar, and pepper, if needed. Serve immediately.

4 to 6 shiitake mushrooms or dried Chinese mushrooms, stems removed

4 cups vegetable stock

1/2 cup sliced bamboo shoots, cut into thin strips

1/2 cup sliced carrot, cut into thin strips

1/2 cup thinly sliced onion

2 tablespoons Shaoxing rice wine or sherry

2 tablespoons rice vinegar

1 tablespoon light soy sauce

1 tablespoon vegetable base (flavor enhancer or bouillon)

1 teaspoon ground white pepper

1/2 teaspoon salt

1 cup firm tofu, well drained and diced

1/4 cup rich soymilk, for a cloudy white soup (optional)

Asian Fusion

Steamed Tofu with Ginger
Si Dau Fu

Serves 6

Steaming is a very practical technique used in Chinese cooking; it is also popular throughout Asia. The Chinese invented many kinds of steamers, which basically consist of a pot for boiling water, one or more well-fitting steam trays that sit on top of the pot, and a tight-fitting lid. Steamers may be made of clay, bamboo, and/or metal. A steamer set can also be made with a wok by using a tray or plate that fits comfortably over the wok and a lid to keep the steam circulating around the food.

C ut the tofu into 1-inch-thick pieces, 2 to 3 inches long. Arrange on a heat-resistant plate that fits comfortably in a streamer tray.

If using the mushrooms, soak them in warm water for 10 to 15 minutes, or until soft. Squeeze out excess water and trim the tough stems. Arrange the mushrooms over the tofu. Sprinkle with the salt-and-pepper mixture. Let stand for at least 5 to 10 minutes.

Combine the soy sauce, wine, vegetable oil, sesame oil, and optional sugar in a small bowl. Pour evenly over the tofu. Sprinkle with the ginger and green onions.

Place the steamer over high heat and bring the water to a full boil. Place the plate of tofu on the streamer tray, cover with a tight-fitting lid, and steam for 10 to 15 minutes, or until heated through (about 10 minutes for each inch of thickness of tofu). Serve immediately, while still hot.

1 pound silken tofu, well drained

6 dried black mushrooms (optional)

$1/4$ teaspoon salt and $1/4$ teaspoon ground pepper, mixed

2 tablespoons light soy sauce or seasoning soy sauce (such as Maggi Seasoning Sauce or mushroom-flavored soy sauce)

2 tablespoons Shaoxing rice wine or sherry

2 teaspoons vegetable oil

1 teaspoon sesame oil

1 teaspoon sugar (optional)

$1/4$ cup peeled and matchstick-sliced fresh ginger

$1/4$ cup thinly sliced green onions, both green and white parts

Tofu-Sheet Wraps
Chai Siu Ngo

Serves 6

Fresh tofu sheets, or bean curd skins, come in large pieces wrapped in plastic and are available refrigerated or frozen. Dried tofu sheets can be found in the dry goods aisle of Asian grocery stores. They are large and unmistakable, like a bag of bath towels; you can't miss them. They are used mainly as wrappers, but they are also cut up and included in many other dishes, such as in stir-fries, soups, and salads. Dried tofu sheets need to be rehydrated in liquid before using so they are pliable for wrapping. Like most fried foods, these wraps are best when served hot; fried tofu sheets become tough when cold.

8 to 10 dried shiitake or black mushrooms

1³/₄ cups (one 14-ounce can) vegetable stock or the soaking liquid from the mushrooms

2 tablespoons light soy sauce

2 tablespoons Shaoxing rice wine or sherry

1 teaspoon sesame oil

3 tofu sheets (bean curd skins), each at least 8 x 12 inches

2 cups matchstick-sliced carrots

2 cups matchstick-sliced celery

¹/₄ cup dark soy sauce, plus more as needed

1 tablespoon sugar

¹/₂ teaspoon ground pepper

¹/₄ cup vegetable oil, plus more as needed

Soak the mushrooms in warm water for 15 to 20 minutes, or until soft. Drain and squeeze out the excess water. Trim and discard the tough stems. Slice the mushrooms into very thin strips.

Combine the vegetable stock, light soy sauce, wine, and sesame oil in a bowl.

Lay the tofu sheets in a tray and pour the stock mixture over them. Soak the tofu sheets for 5 to 7 minutes, or until they are pliable enough to be folded and rolled.

To assemble the wraps, work with 1 tofu sheet at a time. Spread 1 tofu sheet on a large tray. Scatter about one-third of the carrots and celery thinly over one-half of the sheet. Sprinkle with some of the dark soy sauce, sugar, and pepper. Fold the other half of the sheet over the vegetables. Scatter a thin layer of mushrooms over the sheet and sprinkle again with some of the dark soy sauce, sugar, and pepper.

Fold the sheet three times so the wrap is about one-third of the previous size. Repeat the same process with the remaining 2 tofu sheets. Brush all of the wraps with more of the dark soy sauce.

To fry the wraps, heat the oil in a large pan over medium heat. Add 1 wrap and fry it for 3 to 4 minutes, turning it occasionally, until the outside is golden brown and crispy all over. Remove the wrap from the pan and place it on a rack or on absorbent paper to drain the oil. Fry the remaining wraps the same way.

Cut the wraps into 2-inch-long pieces. Serve immediately, while still warm and soft.

Tomato Salad
Chung Sik Faan Ke Sa Leut

Serves 6

Traveling a long way from the Aztecs of South America to Europe and then to Asia, this fruit of love, pomme d'amour *("love apple" in French) or* pomodoro *("tomato" in Italian), is adored by all Asian cuisines. Exactly how and when this recipe came about is hard to discern, although Italians have a similar dish involving cheese and basil. The Chinese successfully grow plump and delicious tomatoes, including many heirloom varieties. When in season, tomatoes are best served fresh. Sometimes other fresh fruits are added to this salad to vary the taste and texture.*

3 large, ripe tomatoes

3 tablespoons thinly sliced green onion, both green and white parts

2 tablespoons rice vinegar

1 tablespoon minced garlic

1 tablespoon light soy sauce

1 teaspoon sugar, more or less to taste

1 teaspoon sesame oil

$1/2$ teaspoon salt, or more to taste

$1/2$ teaspoon ground pepper

Slice the tomatoes thinly and arrange them on a serving platter. Refrigerate to chill.

To make the dressing, combine the remaining ingredients in a bowl and stir to mix well. To serve, sprinkle the dressing evenly over the tomatoes.

Vegetarian Spring Rolls

Sou Choi Cheun Gyun

Makes 20; serves 6

Spring roll dishes are designed to take full advantage of the best produce that each season has to offer. Reap your garden's bounties and make delicious spring rolls all year long.

2 to 3 ounces dried cellophane or bean thread noodles
6 to 8 fresh shiitake mushrooms
1 tablespoon vegetable oil
1 tablespoon sesame oil
2 tablespoons peeled and minced fresh ginger
2 tablespoons minced garlic (optional)
1 cup matchstick-sliced carrot
1 cup matchstick-sliced green cabbage
4 ounces fried or firm tofu, sliced into thin strips
2 tablespoons thinly sliced green onion, both green and white parts
2 tablespoons light soy sauce
2 tablespoons sugar, more or less to taste
1 tablespoon vegetable base (flavor enhancer or bouillon cube)
1/2 teaspoon ground pepper
24 pieces fresh spring roll or frozen lumpia wrappers (8 inches square)
3 cups vegetable oil, for frying
1 bottle soy sauce, for dipping
1 bottle ready-made sweet-and-sour chile sauce, for dipping

Soak the noodles in warm water for 15 to 20 minutes, or until soft. Drain the noodles and cut them into 3-inch threads.

Twist off and discard tough stems of the mushrooms. Slice the caps into thin strips.

To make the filling, heat the tablespoon of vegetable oil and sesame oil in a wok over high heat. Stir in the ginger and optional garlic. Cook and stir for 1 to 2 minutes, until light brown and fragrant. Add the mushrooms, carrot, cabbage, tofu, and green onion. Stir to combine well. Cook and stir for 1 to 2 minutes. Add the noodles, soy sauce, sugar, vegetable base, and pepper. Stir to mix well. Cook and stir for 1 to 2 minutes longer. Do not overcook the mixture or the vegetables will release too much liquid. Spread the mixture on a tray in a thin layer and let cool.

To wrap a spring roll, arrange a wrapper on a flat surface with one pointed corner toward you. Put about 2 tablespoons of the filing just above the pointed side into a 4-inch-long log. Fold the pointed tip over the filling and roll once to secure. Fold in both side ends of the wrapper tightly and continue to roll and seal the opposite tip with a little water. Repeat the process to make more spring rolls.

Heat the oil in a wok or deep pan to 375 degrees F. The oil should have a depth of at least 2 inches. Make sure that the oil is hot before cooking the spring rolls. Fill the pan loosely with spring rolls. Fry the rolls, turning them occasionally, for 4 to 5 minutes, or until they are golden brown and crispy all over. Transfer the spring rolls to a rack or absorbent paper to drain the oil.

Serve the spring rolls hot, with the soy sauce and sweet-and-sour sauce in separate bowls to pass at the table.

India

Baked Spiced-Bread Dessert
Shahi Tukda

Serves 6

Bread has become universal, and different cuisines have adapted bread into various versions with their ingredients and cooking applications. There is a wide spectrum of bread in terms of taste, texture, color, and base ingredients. Leftover bread is sometimes given a new life in the form of delicious desserts, such as bread pudding. Indian cooks are no less ingenious, adding a trademark of their native cookery with various spices, especially saffron, which makes this dessert unique.

Toast the saffron in a dry pot over medium heat for 1 to 2 minutes, until fragrant (take care that it doesn't burn). Stir in the coconut cream, chopped fruits, sugar, cardamom seeds, and cinnamon stick. Continue cooking until the liquid is bubbling around the edges of the pot. Remove from the heat and set aside.

Preheat the oven to 400 degrees F. Lightly oil a baking dish or casserole dish that is large enough and deep enough to hold all the bread and sauce.

Lightly oil a large pan over medium heat. Toast the bread pieces in the pan in a single layer until lightly brown and crisp on both sides. Add more oil and repeat the process until all the bread is toasted.

Arrange the bread pieces in the baking pan, overlapping them. Pour the fruit mixture over all of the pieces. Bake for 15 to 20 minutes, until the top is golden brown.

Sprinkle with the nutmeg. Serve warm, with the whipped cream.

See photo facing page 32.

1/2 teaspoon saffron threads

1 1/2 cups coconut cream

1 cup chopped mixed dried fruits of your choice (such as apricots, figs, and mangoes)

1/4 cup sugar, or more to taste

3 cardamom pods, cracked for seeds

1 cinnamon stick

1/4 cup vegetable oil, plus more as needed

6 to 8 slices white bread, crusts trimmed, cut into 16 (2-inch) triangles

1/2 teaspoon grated nutmeg, for garnish

1 cup nondairy whipped cream

Cucumber Raita

Raita

Serves 6

Spicy Indian foods sometimes overwhelm the sensibility of taste buds. Raitas, which come in many variations, are designed to be a cooling counterbalance to a number of spicy dishes. The most popular raita uses cucumber as a natural cooling agent; however, other vegetables and fruits can be used, such as eggplants, potatoes, spinach, tomatoes, or bananas. For an even more cooling effect, chill the dish before serving.

1 large hothouse cucumber
1 teaspoon whole coriander seeds
1 teaspoons whole fennel seeds
1/2 teaspoon whole cumin seeds (optional)
1 pound very soft silken tofu, well drained
1/4 cup chopped fresh mint leaves
3 tablespoons freshly squeezed lime or lemon juice, or more to taste
1 green jalape–o or serrano chile, seeded and minced
1/2 teaspoon salt, or more to taste
1/2 teaspoon ground black pepper
6 Indian papadums (crackers)

Wash the cucumber and cut it in half lengthwise. If the seeds are large and hard, scoop them out with a spoon and discard them. Thinly slice the cucumber crosswise into half-moons. If desired, to get rid of excess moisture, put the slices in a bowl, sprinkle them with a little salt, and toss gently. Let sit for 4 to 5 minutes. Rinse with cold water and lightly squeeze out the liquid.

Combine the coriander, fennel, and optional cumin seeds in a dry pan over medium heat. Roast, swirling the pan occasionally, for 3 to 4 minutes, until the seeds are fragrant. Grind the seeds in a mortar with pestle or process them into a powder in a spice grinder.

Place the drained tofu in a bowl. Using a wire whisk, beat it until smooth. Stir in the ground seeds, cucumber, mint leaves, lime juice, chile, salt, and pepper. Add more lime juice and other seasonings to taste.

To cook the papadums, heat 3 cups of vegetable oil in a deep pan to 375 degrees F. The oil should have a depth of at least 2 inches. If each papadum is too big to fit in the pan, break it into smaller portions. Fry each papadum in the hot oil until golden brown, fully expanded, and bubbly on the surface. Transfer to a rack or absorbent paper to drain the oil.

Serve the warm papadums with the raita (like chips and dip). Alternatively, serve the raita as a side dish to Indian curries or spicy dishes (with or without the papadums).

Dosa Masala
Masala Dosa

Serves 6

Masala is an Indian spice blend with a minimum combination of three spices, such as cardamom, coriander, and mace; it can also be a complex blend with ten or more ingredients. Ready-made masala is available at Indian grocery stores; or, if you feel inventive, choose your favorite Indian spices and make your own blend. All dried spices should be roasted in a dry pan (on the stove or in the oven) to intensify their flavors and turn them brittle and crunchy, which makes them easy to grind into a powder. Serve this dish with ready-made Indian dosas, which are available fresh or in the frozen-foods section at Indian or Asian markets.

Heat the oil in a large pan over medium heat. Stir in the mustard seeds and cook for 2 to 3 minutes, until they start to jump and crackle. Stir in the onions, curry leaves, and chiles. Cook, stirring frequently, for 4 to 6 minutes, or until the onions are light brown and soft.

Stir in the potatoes, masala, turmeric, and salt. Pour in the water and bring to a boil. Decrease the heat to low, cover with a lid, and simmer for 13 to 15 minutes, until the potatoes are tender and most of the water has evaporated. Stir in the coconut cream, cilantro, tamarind paste, sugar, and vegetable base. Add more coconut cream if the mixture is too dry. Adjust the seasonings to taste.

To serve, fill the dosas with the potato mixture and roll them like a tortilla. Serve hot, with your choice of chutney on the side.

3 tablespoons mustard oil or vegetable oil

1 tablespoon black mustard seeds

2 cups chopped yellow onions

12 fresh curry leaves, or 1 to 2 tablespoons dried curry leaves

3 tablespoons chopped green jalape–o or serrano chiles

1$^1/2$ pounds new potatoes, scrubbed and diced

2 teaspoons masala or garam masala

1 teaspoon ground turmeric

$1/2$ teaspoon salt, or more to taste

1 cup water, plus more as needed

$1/2$ cup coconut cream, plus more as needed

$1/4$ cup chopped fresh cilantro leaves, plus more for garnish

1 tablespoon tamarind paste or liquid, or more to taste

1 tablespoon sugar, or more to taste

1 tablespoon vegetable base (flavor enhancer or bouillon cube)

8 Indian dosas or other soft, thin bread, kept warm

1 cup chutney of your choice

Eggplant, Cauliflower, and Green Bean Korma
Sabzi Ka Korma

Serves 6

Korma, *a cooking technique like braising or stewing, originated in Turkey, traveled through the Middle East, and entered North India. Now it has become popular in Indian curry dishes of slow-cooked vegetables, with the addition of various nuts, rich coconut cream, or tofu. A variety of spices is added to make the dish more regional, or in this case, more personal, with our favorite spices. Serve it with steamed rice or your choice of Indian bread and chutney.*

Grind and pound the cashew nuts, garlic, and ginger in a mortar with pestle or process them into a paste in a food processor. Add the cardamom and cinnamon stick and grind lightly, just enough to crush the spices. (Do not overprocess them into small pieces, as they will be difficult for your guests to pick out and avoid when eating.)

Heat the oil in a large pan or pot over medium heat. Add the onions and cook and stir for 3 to 5 minutes, until golden brown. Stir in the cashew nut paste, garam masala, and turmeric. Cook and stir for 2 to 4 minutes, until fragrant.

Stir in the coconut cream, water, and potatoes and bring to a boil. Decrease the heat, cover with a lid, and cook for 4 to 6 minutes. Stir in the cauliflower, eggplant, green beans, vegetable base, salt, and pepper. Cover and cook, stirring occasionally, for 4 to 5 minutes, or until all the vegetables are tender. Add more coconut cream or water as needed to prevent the mixture from burning on the bottom of the pan. Adjust the seasonings to taste. Transfer to a serving bowl. Garnish with the cilantro and mint.

1/3 cup roasted cashew nuts

2 tablespoons chopped garlic

2 tablespoons peeled and chopped fresh ginger

5 to 6 whole cardamom pods

1 cinnamon stick

1/4 cup vegetable oil

1 1/2 cups chopped yellow onions

1 teaspoon garam masala

1/2 teaspoon ground turmeric

1 1/2 cups coconut cream or coconut milk, plus more as needed

1/2 cup water, plus more as needed

1/3 pound potatoes, peeled and diced

1/3 pound cauliflower, cut into small florets

1/3 pound eggplant, diced

1/3 pound green beans, cut into 1/2-inch-long sticks

1 tablespoon vegetable base (flavor enhancer or bouillon)

1/2 teaspoon salt, or more to taste

1/2 teaspoon ground pepper

1/4 cup chopped fresh cilantro leaves, for garnish

1/4 cup chopped fresh mint leaves, for garnish

Lentil-and-Spinach Dal
Palak Dal

Serves 6

Dal *refers to Indian lentils or the dishes that are made with them. This version of dal has spinach added. Assorted spices are essential for obtaining the complex, aromatic flavors. Other spices of your choice can be used, adding to or replacing the listed ingredients and personalizing the dish to make it your own. As dried beans take a while to cook and fresh spinach cooks very quickly, make sure that the lentils have just the right texture before adding the spinach for the final touch.*

See photo facing page 33.

$\frac{1}{4}$ cup vegetable oil

2 teaspoons black mustard seeds

2 green jalape–o or serrano chiles, cut lengthwise into quarters

$\frac{1}{4}$ cup peeled and minced fresh ginger

1$\frac{1}{2}$ cups split yellow lentils, split yellow peas, or split chana dal

6 cups vegetable stock or water

1 tablespoon vegetable base (flavor enhancer or bouillon cube)

1 tablespoon sugar, or more to taste

2 teaspoons ground cumin

2 teaspoons ground coriander

1 teaspoon ground turmeric

$\frac{1}{2}$ teaspoon asafetida

$\frac{1}{2}$ teaspoon salt

1 pound fresh spinach, leaves only

1 cup thinly sliced green onions, both green and white parts

Heat the oil in a pot over medium heat. Stir in the mustard seeds, chiles, and ginger. Cook for 2 to 3 minutes, until the mustard seeds start to jump and crackle and the chiles sizzle. Transfer to a bowl and set aside for garnish.

Rinse the lentils thoroughly with cold water. Put the lentils and vegetable stock in the same pot used for the mustard seeds and bring to a boil over high heat. Decrease the heat to low and cook for 8 to 10 minutes, skimming off any foam or impurities that float to the surface.

Stir in the vegetable base, sugar, cumin, coriander, turmeric, asafetida, and salt. Partially cover the pot with a lid and simmer for 35 to 40 minutes, until the lentils are very tender and only a little liquid is left on top.

Stir in the spinach and green onions. Cook for 4 to 6 minutes, until the spinach is wilted. Add a little water if the mixture is too dry. Adjust the seasonings to taste.

Transfer to a serving platter. Sprinkle with the reserved mustard seeds, chiles, and ginger for garnish.

Mango Chutney
Aam Ki Chutney

Makes about 2 cups

Mango is the most popular ingredient in chutney, both in India and worldwide, because of its unique taste and tropical flavor. If available, green mango provides a sour note and crunchy texture. There are many varieties of mango, each uniquely different in taste, texture, and color, and most are suitable for chutney. Choose a mango that is firm and not fully ripe because ripe flesh will fall apart after being cooked. If you are unable to eat mango because of an allergy to it, choose local, seasonal fruits with a similar texture to mango, such as firm apricots.

1 large mango (1 pound), peeled, pitted, and finely chopped

3 tablespoons freshly squeezed lime or lemon juice

1 tablespoon vegetable oil

1/4 cup chopped shallots

2 tablespoons minced garlic

2 tablespoons thinly sliced green jalape–o or serrano chiles

1 tablespoon peeled and minced fresh ginger

1 teaspoon black mustard seeds

1 teaspoon whole coriander seeds

1/3 cup palm or brown sugar, or more to taste

1/3 cup white wine vinegar

1 teaspoon salt, or more to taste

Combine the mango and lime juice in a glass or ceramic bowl and set aside.

Heat the oil in a pan over medium-high heat. Stir in the shallots, garlic, chiles, and ginger. Cook for 2 to 3 minutes, until light brown and fragrant. Add the mustard and coriander seeds and cook and stir for 2 minutes.

Stir in the mango (including the lime juice), sugar, vinegar, and salt. Stir to mix well. Decrease the heat to low and simmer for about 10 minutes, until the mixture thickens and the mango is well coated with a syrupy sauce.

Remove from the heat and let cool completely. Store in a covered container in the refrigerator and use within 1 week.

Parathas

Parathas

Makes 10 pieces; serves 6

The easiest Indian breads, such as this one, require only kneading and resting. Choose your spices and modify the amount of seasonings to your liking. Like any other dough, its texture depends on the ratio of liquid to flour, so make adjustments accordingly—more liquid if it's too dry, more flour if it's too wet.

1½ cups whole wheat flour, plus more for dusting

¾ teaspoon salt

1 teaspoon spice of your choice, such as whole cumin seeds, black mustard seeds, or a mix (optional)

1 tablespoon sugar (optional)

¾ cup water, plus more as needed

⅔ cup vegetable oil, plus more as needed

Sift together the flour, salt, and optional spice and sugar in a mixing bowl. Gradually stir in enough water to make a stiff dough. Transfer to a lightly floured surface and knead the dough for 8 to 10 minutes, until smooth and elastic. Return the dough to the bowl, cover with a damp towel, and let rest for 20 minutes.

Divide the dough into 10 equal balls. Roll out each ball with a rolling pin on a lightly floured surface into a 4-inch circle. Brush the circle with a generous amount of the oil, and then fold the circle in half and brush it with more oil. Fold it in half again to form a triangle, and then press the layers together. Roll out the triangle into a larger piece, almost double the size. Cover with a damp towel. Roll out the remaining balls of dough using the same process.

Heat a dry skillet over high heat until very hot (a splash of water should glide across the surface). Cook 1 paratha at a time. Place the paratha in the pan and cook until bubbles appear on the surface. Press the paratha down flat with a spatula so it cooks evenly. Turn the paratha over and brush it with a little oil. Turn it over again and brush it with more oil. Continue cooking until all sides are golden brown. Brush with more oil.

Serve the parathas hot from the skillet, or wrap them in foil to keep them warm for up to 20 minutes.

Spicy Tomato Raita
Tamattar Ka Raita

Serves 6

Tomatoes are universal now and very popular throughout India. This raita, made with cooked tomatoes, can be served chilled. It is a good accompaniment to spicy dishes and will help offset the heat.

Heat the oil in a pan over medium heat. Stir in the mustard seeds and cook for 2 to 3 minutes, until they start to jump and crackle. Stir in the shallots, garlic, ginger, and dried chiles. Cook for 3 to 4 minutes, until the mixture is fragrant.

Stir in the green chiles, curry leaves, coriander, and turmeric. Then stir in the tomatoes and tomato paste. Decrease the heat to low and simmer, stirring occasionally, for 4 to 5 minutes.

Remove the pan from the heat and gently beat in the tofu, lemon juice, chopped mint, sugar, and salt, making sure that the mixture is smooth and well combined. Adjust the seasonings to taste. Transfer to a serving bowl, and garnish with whole mint leaves.

2 tablespoons vegetable oil

1 teaspoon black mustard seeds

1/3 cup thinly sliced shallots

2 tablespoons minced garlic

2 tablespoons peeled and minced fresh ginger

2 small dried chiles

1/4 cup minced green jalape–o or serrano chiles, more or less to taste

12 fresh curry leaves

1 teaspoon ground coriander

1/2 teaspoon ground turmeric

1 pound large, ripe tomatoes, chopped

2 tablespoons tomato paste

1 1/2 cups silken tofu, well drained

1/4 cup freshly squeezed lemon or lime juice

1/4 chopped fresh mint leaves, plus additional whole leaves for garnish

1 teaspoon sugar

1/2 teaspoon salt, or more to taste

Stuffed Eggplants
Bharwan Naingan Tamattari

Serves 6

Asia grows a variety of eggplants, both large and small, purple and green, and firm and soft. Any eggplants from your local farmers market or grocery store can be used, just take into account their cooking time, as most Asian eggplants have a denser texture and take longer to cook than standard eggplants. Serve this dish hot, with raita and Indian bread or steamed rice on the side.

To make the stuffing, roast the coriander, cumin, and fennel seeds in a dry pan over medium heat for 3 to 4 minutes, until they are fragrant and start to jump and crackle. Let cool.

Grind and pound the roasted seeds into a powder in a mortar with pestle. Alternatively, grind them in a food processor. Add the garlic, ginger, and chiles and continue grinding or processing until the mixture turns into a thick paste.

Transfer the paste to a mixing bowl and add the tomatoes, onions, lemon juice, cilantro, vegetable base, sugar, turmeric, and salt. Stir to mix well. The stuffing should be fairly thick.

Stuffing

2 tablespoons whole coriander seeds

1 tablespoon whole cumin seeds

1 tablespoon whole fennel seeds

2 tablespoons chopped garlic

2 tablespoons peeled and chopped fresh ginger

2 tablespoons chopped red chiles, more or less to taste

4 cups seeded and minced tomatoes (about 4 large tomatoes)

2 cups minced yellow onions

1 small lemon or lime, juiced

1/4 cup minced fresh cilantro leaves

1 tablespoon vegetable base (flavor enhancer or bouillon cube)

1 tablespoon sugar

1 teaspoon ground turmeric

1 teaspoon salt, or more to taste

Wash the eggplants with cold water and pat dry. Using the tip of a knife, cut 3 lengthwise slits in each eggplant without cutting through the stem end, so that each eggplant has 4 equal, parallel slices, with the stem holding the slices together.

Spread each eggplant into a fan shape and spread each piece with some of the stuffing. Carefully layer the 4 pieces on top of each other so the eggplant looks whole again.

Spread the oil over the bottom of a pan and place over medium-low heat. Arrange the stuffed eggplants in a single layer in the pan. Cover with a lid and cook for 10 to 12 minutes. Carefully turn the eggplants, cover, and continue cooking for an additional 10 to 12 minutes, or until the eggplants are tender. Check the eggplants occasionally to make sure they are not burning on the bottom of the pan; add a little water, if necessary.

Carefully transfer the eggplants to a serving platter. Garnish with the fresh mint leaves.

Eggplants and Garnish

6 medium Asian long purple eggplants
1/4 cup vegetable oil
3 sprigs fresh mint leaves, for garnish

Turmeric Soymilk Soup
Haldi Dahi Ka Shorba

Serves 6

This rich soup is colored gold with turmeric and is aromatic with other spices. Its base and thickness come from besan (also called gram flour or chana flour), a flour ground from chana dal, a bean similar to chickpeas. Besan is unique to Indian cuisine. The richer the soymilk, the tastier and more satisfying the soup.

1 tablespoon vegetable oil

1 teaspoon whole cumin seeds

1 teaspoon black mustard seeds

1 teaspoon whole fenugreek seeds

4 fresh, hot red chiles, lightly chopped, more or less to taste

2 bay leaves

$1/2$ cup Indian besan, chickpea, or gram flour

1 teaspoon ground turmeric

1 teaspoon salt

1 teaspoon sugar

3 cups vegetable stock

2 cups rich soymilk

Heat the oil in a pot over medium-high heat. Stir in the cumin seeds, mustard seeds, fenugreek seeds, chiles, and bay leaves. Cook and stir for 1 minute or less, until fragrant. Remove the pan from the heat. Take out half of the spice mixture and it set aside for garnish.

Add the besan, turmeric, salt, and sugar to the pan. Whisk in the vegetable stock and soymilk, beating thoroughly until all lumps are gone and the mixture is smooth.

Return the pan to the heat and bring the mixture to a boil, whisking constantly. Decrease the heat to low and simmer, whisking frequently, for 8 to 10 minutes, until the soup thickens and is fully cooked. Taste and make sure the flour is cooked. Adjust the flavor with more salt and sugar to taste. Add more soymilk or vegetable stock to achieve the desired consistency.

Ladle the soup into bowls. Top with the reserved spice mixture for garnish.

Indonesia

Baked Eggplants with Coconut

Pepes

Serves 6

This classical dish originated in Java island, where Jakarta, the capital city of Indonesia, is located. Various regional versions of this dish are served everywhere and have become the Indonesian specialty, particularly in Javanese cuisine. Wrapping and baking the eggplant in banana leaves provides a hint of sweet, smoky flavor and an authentic appearance, which adds a tropical feel to the dish. Serve the wraps whole and let your dinner guests have fun unwrapping them and discovering the special treat inside.

3 tablespoons vegetable oil

$1/4$ cup minced lemongrass, tender midsection only

3 tablespoons seeded and minced red jalape-o or serrano chiles

3 tablespoons minced shallots

2 tablespoons minced garlic

2 tablespoons peeled and minced fresh ginger

$1 1/2$ cups grated fresh coconut or dried coconut flakes

1 cup fresh mint leaves

1 cup vegetable stock or water

$1/4$ cup tamarind liquid, or more to taste

2 tablespoons light soy sauce

1 tablespoon sugar, or more to taste

1 tablespoon vegetable base (flavor enhancer or bouillon cube)

1 teaspoon ground coriander

$1/2$ teaspoon chile powder

$1/2$ teaspoon salt, or more to taste

1 package banana leaves or parchment paper

6 large Asian long purple eggplants (1 to $1 1/2$ pounds)

Heat the oil in a pan over medium heat. Add the lemongrass, chiles, shallots, garlic, and ginger and cook and stir for 3 to 4 minutes, until light brown and fragrant. Stir in the coconut, mint leaves, vegetable stock, tamarind liquid, soy sauce, sugar, vegetable base, coriander, chile powder, and salt. Decrease the heat to low and simmer for 8 to 10 minutes (the consistency should be similar to tomato sauce). If the sauce is too thick, add a little more stock or water. Adjust the seasonings to taste. Turn off the heat.

Preheat the oven to 350 degrees F.

Cut the banana leaves into 12 (12-inch) squares, stacking 2 pieces for each wrapper. Alternatively, cut the parchment paper into 6 (12-inch) squares, using 1 piece per wrapper.

Trim the eggplants and slice them in half lengthwise. Cut each half into several 2-inch strips. Add the eggplant strips to the coconut sauce and toss to mix well. Divide the eggplant into 6 portions, and put each portion in the middle of a banana wrap or piece of parchment paper. Pull all edges of each wrapper on top of the eggplant into a bundle and secure with a strip of banana leaf or paper or a toothpick.

Arrange the wraps on a baking sheet. Bake for 20 to 25 minutes, or until the eggplant is tender.

To serve, put each wrap on a dinner plate. Serve the wraps sealed, so they stay warm until your guests open them.

Fried Rice
Nasi Goreng

Serves 6

Leftover, cold, and semidry rice is suitable for this dish, as it absorbs all the flavors better. If using freshly cooked rice, crumble and spread it on a tray for two to three hours to cool completely, or refrigerate it to cool. Fried rice is an easy, practical, and popular one-dish meal.

See photo facing page 73.

3 tablespoons vegetable oil

3 tablespoons minced garlic

1 cup thinly sliced yellow onion

1 cup finely diced carrot

1 cup thinly sliced green beans or long beans, cut into ¼-inch-long sticks

1 cup finely diced colorful bell peppers

3 cups cooked or steamed rice (prepared from 1½ cups uncooked rice), or 3 cups chilled leftover rice, crumbled

3 tablespoons sugar, or more to taste

2 tablespoons light soy sauce

2 tablespoons *kecap manis* (Indonesian sweet soy sauce)

2 tablespoons vegetarian stir-fry sauce

2 tablespoons *sambal oelek* (Indonesian hot chile sauce), more or less to taste

1 tablespoon vegetable base (flavor enhancer or bouillon cube)

Heat the oil in a wok over high heat. Add the garlic and cook and stir for 1 to 2 minutes, until light brown and fragrant. Stir in the onion, carrot, green beans, and bell peppers. Cook and stir for 2 to 3 minutes, until the vegetables are cooked through.

Stir in the rice and mix until thoroughly combined. Sprinkle with the sugar, soy sauce, *kecap manis*, stir-fry sauce, *sambal oelek*, and vegetable base. Cook and stir for 2 to 3 minutes, until all of the ingredients are evenly distributed and the mixture is even in color and heated through. Adjust the seasonings to taste. Transfer to a serving platter. Serve hot.

Corn Fritters
Pergedel Jagung

Serves 6

Golden nuggets of corn were first brought to Asia by Portuguese and Spanish fleets in the sixteenth century. Now corn is cultivated as a cash crop almost everywhere and has been hybridized into several delicious varieties. This recipe combines ingredients from both the New and Old Worlds, with plenty of local spices from the Spice Islands of Indonesia. The cooked fritters keep well, wrapped tightly and stored in the freezer for a couple of months. Defrost and reheat them for one to two minutes before serving.

To make the fritters, slice the whole corn kernels off the cobs. Combine the corn with the tofu, shallots, green onion, cornstarch, vegetable base, coriander, baking powder, salt, chile powder, and optional cloves in a mixing bowl. Gently toss to mix well, making sure there are no large clumps of the tofu.

Gently add the flour, a little at a time, to make a fritter dough thick enough to form patties. Add more flour if necessary.

Heat about one-third of the oil in a skillet over medium heat. When the oil is hot, spoon about 1 heaping tablespoon of the fritter dough into the pan. Spoon in additional fritters (using 1 heaping tablespoon of dough per fritter) to fit the pan loosely. Flatten the fritters with a spatula or spoon to about ¼ inch thick. Cook for 2 to 3 minutes on each side, turning once, until the fritters are golden brown and cooked through. Transfer the fritters to a rack or absorbent paper to drain the oil. Add more oil to the pan, if necessary, and make more fritters.

Serve the hot fritters with Chile Soy Sauce (page 69), Cucumber Dipping Sauce (page 143), or ready-made sweet chile sauce.

Corn Fritters

6 ears fresh sweet corn (5 to 6 cups of kernels)

¼ pound silken tofu, well drained and mashed (¼ to ⅓ cup)

3 tablespoons chopped shallots

2 tablespoons chopped green onion, green part only

2 tablespoons cornstarch

1 tablespoon vegetable base (flavor enhancer or bouillon cube)

2 teaspoons ground coriander

1½ teaspoons baking powder

1 teaspoon salt, or more to taste

½ teaspoon chile powder, more or less to taste

¼ teaspoon ground cloves (optional)

¼ to ⅓ cup all-purpose flour, plus more as needed

½ cup vegetable oil for frying, plus more as needed

To make the sauce, combine the sugar and soy sauce in a small pot over medium heat. Cook for 2 to 3 minutes, until the sugar is dissolved. Remove from the heat and let cool. Add the tomato paste, vinegar, onion, ginger, and *sambal oelek*. Stir to mix well. If the sauce is too thick, add a little water.

Chile Soy Sauce

Makes 1 cup

1/2 cup brown sugar

1/3 cup soy sauce

2 tablespoons tomato paste or ketchup

2 tablespoons white vinegar

2 tablespoons minced onion

2 tablespoons peeled and minced fresh ginger

1 tablespoon *sambal oelek* (Indonesian chile paste), more or less to taste

Fried Tofu with Lemongrass Sauce
Goreng Sambal Bawang

Serves 6

Lemongrass grows well in tropical climates, and its flavor can be easily infused into food during cooking. When very thinly sliced, its tender inner sections can be eaten directly. In this recipe, the main ingredient and the sauce are prepared separately. So instead of or in addition to tofu, you can use vegetables of your choice, such as eggplants or mushrooms. Cook this dish according to your preference, and then top it off with the sauce.

Pat the tofu slices dry with paper towels. Rub them all over with the turmeric and the salt-and-pepper mixture.

Heat the oil in a pan over medium heat. Fry the tofu slices for 5 to 6 minutes, turning them once or twice, until light brown and crispy on all sides. Transfer the tofu to a serving platter.

Combine the lime juice, lemongrass, shallots, garlic, chiles, kaffir lime leaves, soy sauce, optional fermented bean curds, and sugar in a small bowl. Stir to mix well, until the sugar is completely dissolved.

To serve, spoon the lemongrass sauce over the fried tofu. Serve immediately.

1 pound firm tofu, well drained and cut into 1 x 1 x 4-inch pieces

1 teaspoon ground turmeric

1/4 teaspoon salt and 1/4 teaspoon ground pepper, mixed

1/4 cup vegetable oil

1/4 cup freshly squeezed lime juice

1/4 cup very thinly sliced lemongrass, tender midsection only

3 tablespoons very thinly sliced shallots

2 tablespoons very thinly sliced garlic

2 tablespoons minced Thai or jalape–o chiles, more or less to taste

2 tablespoons very thinly sliced (chiffonade) fresh kaffir lime leaves

2 tablespoons light soy sauce

2 tablespoons fermented bean curds (optional)

1 tablespoon sugar

Spiced Coconut
Serundeng

Serves 6

On an archipelago in a tropical climate like Indonesia, coconut has found an ideal place to flourish, and the local people have domesticated coconut further so it can be grown on large-scale plantations. Coconut products have been used in all aspects of daily life: building materials, apparel, fuel, medicines, cosmetics, oil, and food ingredients. Serundeng, spiced coconut, is a popular side dish and garnish to many Indonesian meals, and it is especially common on buffet tables. These aromatic and crunchy coconut flakes add exciting taste and texture to any dish.

1 whole mature coconut, or 1½ cups unsweetened dried coconut flakes
1 tablespoon whole coriander seeds
1 teaspoon whole cumin seeds
1 whole clove
1 cup minced yellow onion
2 tablespoons minced garlic
2 tablespoons peeled and minced ginger
2 fresh kaffir lime leaves, very thinly sliced (chiffonade)
2 tablespoons vegetable oil
2 tablespoons fermented bean curds (optional)
1 tablespoon sugar
1 teaspoon salt
2 tablespoons freshly squeezed lemon or lime juice
1 cup roasted peanuts

If using a fresh coconut, crack it open in half and drain the coconut juice. With a hand grater, grate the white coconut meat into flakes. Alternatively, ply the white meat from the shell with the tip of a sturdy knife. Shred the white meat with a box grater or process it in a food processor.

Combine the coriander seeds, cumin seeds, and clove in a dry pan over medium heat. Roast the spices, shaking the pan occasionally, for 2 to 3 minutes, until they crackle and become fragrant. Let cool. Grind the spices into a powder in a mortar with pestle or in a food processor. Add the onion, garlic, ginger, kaffir lime leaves, and coconut flakes. Grind and process until well blended.

Heat the oil in a pan over medium heat. Add the coconut mixture. Cook and stir for 3 to 4 minutes, until fragrant. Add the optional fermented bean curds, sugar, and salt.

Decrease the heat to low and continue cooking, stirring frequently, for 12 to 15 minutes, or until dry and crisp.

Remove from the heat. Stir in the lemon juice. Let cool. Add the roasted peanuts and toss until evenly distributed. Serve at once or store in the refrigerator for up to 1 week.

Mushroom Skewers
Satay

Makes 12 to 16 pieces; serves 6

Indonesia is well known for its food on skewers called satay, which is a cooking technique brought along by Arab traders and is based on their kabob. A variety of ingredients that can be cut up, marinated, and skewered are destined to become satay. Satay is available everywhere in Indonesia—at home, at high-end restaurants, and from street vendors. On the street, you can just follow the delectable aroma or trail the smoke from wood-burning grills to easily find the satay.

Mushrooms and Marinade

1 pound portobello mushrooms, stems removed

1 package bamboo skewers (6 inches long), soaked in water for 30 minutes

2 stalks minced lemongrass, tender midsection only (about 1/2 cup)

2 tablespoons minced garlic

2 tablespoons peeled and minced ginger

2 tablespoons minced green onion, green part only

1 tablespoon ground pepper

1 teaspoon salt

Vegetable oil, for brushing

Slice the mushroom caps into 1/2-inch-thick, long strips. Spear each piece with a bamboo skewer, threading the stick through the mushrooms.

Combine the lemongrass, garlic, ginger, and green onion. Rub this marinade mixture over the mushrooms, making sure that all surfaces are covered. Sprinkle the mushrooms with the pepper and salt. Arrange and stack the mushroom skewers in a tray and sprinkle them lightly with vegetable oil. Cover with plastic wrap and set aside to marinate for 8 to 12 hours in the refrigerator or at least 1 hour at room temperature.

Heat a grill pan or prepare a charcoal grill 30 minutes in advance to obtain a medium heat. Grill the mushrooms for 2 to 4 minutes, turning them occasionally, until they are tender. Brush the mushrooms lightly with oil to keep them moist. Serve the mushrooms with Indonesian Peanut Sauce (page 73).

Japanese California-Roll Sushi
(Maki Nori), page 80

Indonesian Fried Rice
(Nasi Goreng), p. 67

Indonesian Peanut Sauce

Satay Sambal

Makes 1½ cups

Peanut sauce is often served with satay. This recipe is extremely easy to make and is commonly prepared in a mortar with pestle. Indonesian mortars are made from flat lava rock, and they come with a cylindrical pestle that rolls and crushes ingredients on the sides of the mortar. Other kinds of mortars with pestles are acceptable, or you could even use a stainless steel bowl with a rolling pin as a makeshift tool.

2 tablespoons minced garlic

2 fresh Thai chiles, more or less to taste

⅓ cup roasted peanuts or peanut paste, or more to taste

¼ cup Indonesian sweet soy sauce (*kecap manis*), or more to taste

¼ cup freshly squeezed lime juice, or more to taste

¼ teaspoon salt, or more to taste

Using a mortar with pestle, crush the garlic and chiles until well blended. Add the peanuts and grind to incorporate them well; the mixture should be almost a paste. Add the soy sauce, lime juice, and salt. Work the pestle and stir until the mixture is well combined. Adjust the seasonings to taste. If the sauce is too thick, add a little water. Alternatively, process all the ingredients in a food processor until well combined, adding a small mount of water as needed to facilitate processing.

Spicy Shredded-Coconut Salad
Urap

Serves 6

Urap *is a prepared salad of fresh and cooked vegetables and is often served as a part of an important feast, such as* selamatan—*a communal meal. The snappy fresh chiles make the refreshing taste pop, contrasting very well with the soothing and creamy fresh coconut. All of the ingredients can be prepared in advance and then tossed together just before serving.*

$1/2$ whole mature coconut, white meat shredded, or
   $1/2$ cup shredded dried coconut
6 ounces baby spinach leaves, washed
6 ounces bean sprouts
4 ounces Chinese long beans or green beans, trimmed
   and cut into 1-inch-long sticks
1 bunch watercress, cleaned and trimmed
$1/4$ cup vegetable oil
$1/4$ cup thinly sliced shallots
2 tablespoons chopped garlic
2 tablespoons chopped Thai or jalape–o chiles, more or
   less to taste
1 tablespoon chopped kaffir lime skin (zest) or fresh
   kaffir lime leaves
2 teaspoons peeled and chopped galangal
2 tablespoons fermented bean curds (optional)
2 tablespoons freshly squeezed lime juice
1 tablespoon light soy sauce
1 tablespoon sugar
$1/4$ teaspoon salt, more or less to taste

If using a fresh coconut, crack it open in half and drain the coconut juice. With a hand grater, grate the white coconut meat into fine strips. Alternatively, ply the white meat from the shell with the tip of a sturdy knife. Shred the white meat with a box grater or process it in a food processor. Set aside.

Bring a pot of water to a boil. Blanch the vegetables, one at a time, in the boiling water until tender (cook the spinach, bean sprouts, and watercress 10 to 12 seconds; cook the long beans for 1 to 2 minutes). Scoop out the vegetables with a slotted spoon or hand strainer and transfer them to a colander. Rinse the vegetables with cold water and drain completely. Set all the vegetables aside in a large bowl in the refrigerator. (If you prefer, some or all of the vegetables can be served raw.)

Heat the oil in a small pan over medium heat. Add the shallots and cook and stir for 3 to 5 minutes, until light brown, fragrant, and crispy, taking care that they do not burn. Drain on absorbent paper. Set aside for garnish.

To make the dressing, grind and pound the garlic, chiles, kaffir lime skin, and galan-gal into a paste in a mortar with pestle. Add the optional fermented bean curds, lime juice, soy sauce, sugar, and salt. Stir to mix well until the sugar is dissolved. Alternatively, process the ingredients in a food processor until well combined.

To serve, gently toss together the coconut, vegetables, and dressing in a mixing bowl. Transfer to a serving platter and garnish with the shallots.

Vegetables Braised in Coconut Juice

Goreng Kalasan

Serves 6

The firm, white meat of mature coconut produces coconut cream and coconut milk. Young coconut, with its soft, underdeveloped, jellylike meat, is popular as a fresh fruit throughout Asia. The juice of young coconut is refreshingly sweet and desirable for quenching one's thirst during the hot and humid months. In this recipe, instead of plain water as a braising element, coconut juice provides an all-in-one liquid with refreshing flavor, sweet taste, coconut fragrance, and essential minerals. Whole young coconuts are available in the refrigerated section of Asian grocery stores, and frozen coconut juice and meat are prepackaged, ready for a number of uses.

1 pound abalone or portobello mushrooms (select large, thick mushrooms)

1 pound fried or firm tofu

$1/4$ teaspoon salt and $1/4$ teaspoon ground pepper, mixed

$1/4$ cup seeded and chopped red jalape-o or serrano chiles

3 tablespoons chopped lemongrass, tender midsection only

3 tablespoons chopped shallots

2 tablespoons chopped garlic

1 teaspoon whole black peppercorns

1 green young coconut, or 2 cups frozen young coconut juice and meat

3 tablespoons vegetable oil

5 to 6 whole fresh kaffir lime leaves

1 to 2 whole salam leaves or bay leaves

2 tablespoons light soy sauce

1 tablespoons vegetable base (flavor enhancer or bouillon cube)

1 teaspoon salt

$1/2$ cup freshly squeezed lime juice

Slice the mushrooms and tofu into $1/2$-inch-thick rectangular pieces. Sprinkle with a little of the salt and pepper mixture. Set aside.

Process the chiles, lemongrass, shallots, garlic, and peppercorns into a smooth paste in a mortar with pestle or in a food processor.

For the fresh coconut, use a heavy clever to chop off the top of the coconut, and then pour the juice into a bowl. With a long-handled spoon, scoop out the tender, white meat of the coconut and mix it with the juice.

Heat the oil in a pot over medium heat. Add the spice paste and cook and stir for 4 to 5 minutes, until fragrant. Add the coconut juice, coconut meat, mushrooms, tofu, kaffir lime leaves, salam leaves, soy sauce, vegetable base, and salt. Bring to a boil. Decrease the heat to medium-low and simmer for 8 to 10 minutes, until the mushrooms are cooked and the sauce has been absorbed and reduced by half.

Just before removing from the heat, stir in the lime juice. Adjust the seasonings to taste. Serve hot.

Fried Tofu Salad and Peanut Dressing
Tahu Goreng

Serves 6

Goreng *is a fried dish often served in Indonesian meals. Many varieties of* goreng *have been recently introduced when new chefs demonstrate their skills. Any ingredients of your choice can be incorporated. Add or subtract the listed ingredients to make this salad your own.*

If using firm tofu, pat it dry with paper towels and cut it into ½-inch cubes. To fry the tofu, heat the oil in a wok or deep pan to 375 degrees F. First fry the shallots for 3 to 5 minutes, until light brown, fragrant, and crispy, taking care that they do not burn. Drain on absorbent papers. Set aside for garnish.

Add the tofu to fit the wok loosely. Fry for 4 to 5 minutes, turning it occasionally, until it is golden brown and crispy. Drain on absorbent paper. Set aside.

If using already fried tofu cubes, fry the shallots in ¼ cup of oil as directed above. Preheat the oven to 375 degrees F. Put the tofu cubes in a pan and warm them in the oven for 10 to 15 minutes, until crispy.

Fill a medium pot with water and bring to a boil. Blanch the bean sprouts in the boiling water for about 30 seconds, and then rinse with them cold water. Set aside.

To serve, combine the beans sprouts, cucumber, carrot, and bell peppers in a bowl. Transfer the vegetables to a serving platter. Top with the fried tofu and sprinkle with the Peanut Dressing (page 77). Garnish with the fried shallots.

Fried Tofu and Vegetables

1 pound firm tofu, well drained, or ½ pound fried tofu cubes

3 cups vegetable oil, for frying the firm tofu, or ¼ cup to fry just the shallots

½ cup thinly sliced shallots

¼ pound bean sprouts

1 cup thinly sliced hothouse cucumber, cut into half-moons

1 cup matchstick-sliced carrot

1 cup matchstick-sliced colorful bell peppers

1 cup Peanut Dressing (page 77)

To make the dressing, grind and pound the peanuts, shallot, garlic, and chiles into a paste in a mortar with pestle. Gradually add the remaining ingredients and mix well, stirring until the sugar is completely dissolved. If the mixture is too thick, add a little water. Adjust the seasonings to taste. Alternatively, process all the ingredients into a paste in a food processor, adding a little water to facilitate processing.

Peanut Dressing

Makes about 1 cup

1/4 to 1/3 cup chopped roasted peanuts

2 tablespoons chopped shallot

2 tablespoons chopped garlic

1 tablespoon chopped Thai or jalape–o chiles, more or less to taste

2 tablespoons sweet soy sauce (*kecap manis*)

2 tablespoons light soy sauce

2 tablespoons palm sugar or brown sugar

1/4 cup tamarind liquid

2 tablespoons freshly squeezed lime or lemon juice

Yellow Rice
Nasi Kuning

Serves 6

Indonesian and Malaysian people celebrate their large or small events with food, and nasi kuning *is always featured. This mound of yellow rice is situated in the center of the buffet table, representing the mountain in the Hindu belief system where supreme beings reign; it is surrounded by dishes and condiments in various sections symbolizing assorted gods, demons, men, and animals. Yellow is a color of luck and higher status (such as royalty), and it is the color of gold, which is popular at any celebratory event. Regular rice or sweet glutinous rice can be used in this recipe. To make the rice creamier, replace the vegetable stock with coconut milk.*

3 tablespoons vegetable oil

2 tablespoons minced shallot

2 cups fragrant rice (such as Thai jasmine or Indian basmati rice)

2 tablespoons ground turmeric

2 tablespoons sugar

1 tablespoon vegetable base (flavor enhancer or bouillon cube)

1 teaspoon ground coriander

1 teaspoon ground cumin

1 teaspoon salt

1 whole cinnamon stick

3 whole cloves

2 whole fresh kaffir lime leaves, dried kaffir lime leaves, or bay leaves

2½ cups vegetable stock or coconut milk

If using a rice cooker, combine all the ingredients in the cooker and follow the manufacturer's instructions to cook the rice.

To cook the rice on the stove, heat the oil in a pot over medium heat. Add the shallot and cook and stir for 1 to 2 minutes, until light brown and fragrant. Add the rice and stir until the grains are well coated with the oil.

Stir in the turmeric, sugar, vegetable base, coriander, cumin, salt, cinnamon stick, cloves, and kaffir lime leaves. Add the vegetable stock and bring to a boil. Decrease the heat to low and cover with a lid. Cook the rice undisturbed for 10 to 15 minutes, until all the liquid has been absorbed and the rice is fully cooked. Turn off the heat and let stand for 5 to 7 minutes on the hot stove.

Fluff the rice and discard the cinnamon, cloves, and kaffir lime leaves before serving.

Japan

California-Roll Sushi
Maki Nori

Serves 6; makes 6 rolls

See photo facing page 72.

This is a modified sushi roll that uses the famous California avocado. The rolling technique requires practice to get the rice and fillings wrapped snuggly. Sushi is one form of Japanese art, and its presentation is as crucial as its taste. Practice makes perfect, and the end result of the sushi roll tells the tale of a sushi maker's skill. To give a spicy, snappy flavor to the sushi, wasabi paste is used. Wasabi is a Japanese version of horseradish derived from the root of wasabi plants. Wasabi is available in both paste and powder forms in most supermarkets. To make your own paste, mix the wasabi powder with cold water using a 1:1 ratio.

3 cups water

2 tablespoons rice vinegar

1/2 pound fried tofu

1 large, ripe avocado

6 toasted nori sheets (each sheet about 4 x 7.5 inches)

3 cups cooked Sushi Rice (page 89)

1/4 cup wasabi paste, or more to taste, plus more for serving

1 bottle sushi or sashimi soy sauce, for serving

Combine the water and rice vinegar in a bowl large enough to fit both hands.

Slice the tofu into long, thin strips. Set aside.

Cut the avocado in half and discard the pit. Peel and slice the avocado lengthwise as thinly as possible, cutting it into long, thin strips.

Place a sheet of nori, shiny-side down, on a sushi mat, with one of the long edges facing you.

Wet both hands in the vinegar water, making sure that both palms are wet. Scoop about 1/3 to 1/2 cup of the rice and mold it loosely into a log. Place the log about 1/2 inch below the top long edge in the center of the nori. Gently spread the rice downward with tips of your fingers into a 1/4-inch-thick layer over three-quarters of the nori.

Evenly distribute 1/6 of the sliced tofu in the middle of the rice, running from the left to right sides of the nori. Top with strips of the avocado, distributing it evenly over the tofu. Spread the wasabi paste to taste evenly on the rice in front of the filling.

With your thumbs under the sushi mat and your fingers holding the filling in place, fold and curl the mat to initiate the roll. Continue rolling and folding, making sure that all of the rice and filling are rolled inside the nori. Gently squeeze along the mat to firm up the roll and shape it into a round log.

Remove the mat and put the sushi roll on a cutting board. Cut the roll in half with a sharp chef's knife, and then slice each half into thirds or quarters to obtain 6 to 8 equal pieces.

Arrange the pieces, cut-side up, on a serving platter. Roll and cut the remaining rice and filling in the same fashion to make 6 rolls in all. Serve the sushi with soy sauce and additional wasabi paste in small saucers on the side.

Green Beans with Sesame Dressing

Saya-ingen Zuke

Serves 6

This cold and crunchy salad is perfect for summer, which is also the best time for tender green beans and asparagus. Snow peas and tender beans are also available. My favorite vegetable for this recipe is fresh baby corn, if you can find it. Canned baby corn is not worth the effort. Fresh corn kernels might be the closest alternative. The vegetables and dressing can be prepared in advance, chilled, and tossed together just before serving.

To cook the green beans or asparagus, fill a pot with 4 to 5 cups of water and bring to a rolling boil over high heat. Parboil the green beans or asparagus for 1 to 2 minutes. Drain and then immediately plunge them into a bowl of ice water to cool. Drain and blot dry. Keep chilled in the refrigerator.

To make the dressing, grind the sesame seeds in a mortar with pestle until they are almost a paste. Add the miso, mirin, sugar, and soy sauce. Stir thoroughly until completely blended and the sugar and miso are dissolved.

Just before serving, toss the beans with the dressing, a little at a time, until the beans are evenly coated. Taste and add more dressing as desired. Transfer to serving plates or bowls. Sprinkle with additional sesame seeds. Serve cold.

Green Beans or Asparagus

3 cups (1 pound) fresh green beans or small baby asparagus, trimmed and cut into 1½-inch-long sticks

Sesame Dressing

Makes about ½ cup

2 tablespoons roasted white and black sesame seeds, plus more for garnish

2 tablespoons white miso (*shiro miso*)

2 tablespoons mirin (cooking sake)

1 tablespoon sugar

1 tablespoon soy sauce

Hot Pot with Udon Noodles
Udon Suki

Serves 6

Japanese hot pots make for fun, family-style feasting, where people gather around a large pot of hot soup and prepare their own delicious bowls, customized to their tastes. A variety of vegetables are cut into bite-sized pieces so they can be easily cooked in the hot, seasoned broth. Hot pots are especially popular for winter feasts, as people snuggle up close, keeping warm with the heat from the pot and each other, and enjoy a healthful meal.

To make the broth, combine all the ingredients in a pot over an electric stove or portable gas stove in the center of the dinning table. Bring to a boil. Adjust the seasonings to taste. Decrease the heat to low and keep warm until serving time.

Arrange the noodles and vegetables (page 83) separately on a platter or on individual plates and place around the hot pot.

For self-service, increase the heat under the broth to high. Each diner selects noodles and vegetables with chopsticks and cooks them in the hot broth. The noodles and vegetables are then returned to the diner's own bowl and the hot broth is ladled over them. Each diner seasons his or her soup with condiments (page 83) to taste.

Broth

8 cups vegetable stock or Seaweed Broth (see Miso Soup, page 84)

3 tablespoons light soy sauce

3 tablespoons mirin (cooking sake)

1 tablespoon vegetable base (flavor enhancer or bouillon cube)

$1/2$ teaspoon salt

$1/2$ teaspoon ground white pepper

To make the noodles, fill another pot with enough water to cook the noodles and bring to a boil. Stir in the noodles and partially cook them: 2 to 4 minutes for fresh noodles and 5 to 6 minutes for dried noodles. Drain. Rinse with cold water and drain again.

Noodles and Vegetables

8 to 10 ounces fresh udon noodles, or 4 to 5 ounces dried udon noodles

2 cups finely diced silken tofu

2 cups matchstick-sliced carrots

2 cups matchstick-sliced snow peas

2 cups sliced napa cabbage, cut into bite-sized pieces

2 cups baby spinach leaves, washed

2 cups thinly sliced shiitake mushrooms

1 cup sliced green onions, both green and white parts, cut into 1-inch lengths

1 cup peeled and finely grated or minced fresh ginger

Condiments

1 lemon, cut into 6 wedges

1 small bottle soy sauce

1 small bottle *ichimi* or *shichimi togarashi* (Japanese dried chile mix; optional)

Miso Soup
Miso Shiru

Serves 6

Requisite skills and years of cumulative knowledge combine to bring about artful and delicious Japanese dishes prepared with perfect execution. Sushi, one form of the Japanese arts, is based on the concept of elegant simplicity. Miso soups often accompany sushi meals, and the concept of simplicity clearly carries through in this recipe. Vegetables of your choice can be used, but consider their cooking times and flavors so that all the ingredients harmonize.

To make broth, wipe the kelp clean with damp paper towels. Combine the water and kelp in a pot and let stand for 30 minutes.

Bring to just a simmer over medium heat (do not bring to a rolling boil). Simmer for 10 to 12 minutes. Remove the kelp using a wire strainer or tongs and discard. Stir the vegetable base into the broth.

To make the soup, heat the broth to almost boiling. Put the miso in a ladle and add some broth to it. Stir to dilute, and then gradually stir the softened miso into the broth. Add the mushrooms, optional mirin, and vegetable base and cook for 3 minutes.

Distribute the tofu, green onions, and nori among serving bowls. Ladle the soup into each bowl and serve.

Seaweed Broth
Dashi

2 to 3 pieces (3 to 4 ounces) dried kelp (*dashi kombu*)

8 cups water

1 tablespoon vegetable or seaweed base (flavor enhancer or bouillon cube)

Soup

5 to 6 cups Seaweed Broth (*dashi*)

1/3 cup white miso (*shiro miso*), or more to taste

2 cups very thinly sliced shiitake mushrooms, tough stems removed

1/2 cup mirin (cooking sake; optional)

1 tablespoon vegetable base (flavor enhancer or bouillon)

1 1/2 cups (1 pound) finely diced silken tofu

1/4 cup finely chopped green onions, both green and white parts

1/4 cup shredded (cut into fine strips) sushi nori

Mixed Vegetable Salad
Shira Ae

Serves 6

This is a common daily salad that goes with any Japanese meal, the same way our green salad is served before an entrée. Any vegetables or even just lettuces of your choice can be used. If you make the dressing thicker, it can be served as a dip, accompanied by cooked and fresh vegetables or various types of chips.

To make the dressing, grind and pound the sesame seeds into a smooth paste in a mortar with pestle. Add the vinegar, mirin, soy sauce, sugar, salt, and pepper. Stir to mix well. Alternatively, combine the ingredients in a blender or food processor and process into a smooth paste.

Add the tofu and process briefly, just until well combined. Transfer to a bowl and refrigerate. Add more vinegar, mirin, soy sauce, or water if the dressing is too thick.

To prepare the vegetables, put 3 to 4 cups of water with little salt in a pot. Bring to a boil over medium heat. Add the asparagus and cook for 2 to 3 minutes, just until tender-crisp. Remove the asparagus with tongs or a wire strainer. Rinse the asparagus with cold water and set aside. Cook the cauliflower and squash the same way and set aside. Do not overcook the vegetables. Drain the radishes.

To serve, arrange the vegetables around the edges of serving bowls. Spoon the dressing in the center of the bowls. Garnish the dressing with the green onions and sesame seeds. Serve cold.

Dressing

1/4 cup roasted white sesame seeds (roast the seeds in a dry pan)

2 tablespoons rice vinegar

2 tablespoons mirin (cooking sake)

1 tablespoon light soy sauce

1 tablespoon sugar

1 teaspoon salt

1/4 teaspoon ground white pepper

1 cup silken tofu (1/2 to 3/4 pound), well drained

Vegetables

6 to 8 asparagus, trimmed and cut into 1 1/2-inch-long strips

1 cup cauliflower or broccoli florets

1 cup julienned yellow squash

1 cup julienned red radishes, soaked in cold water

1 cup julienned colorful bell peppers

1/4 cup thinly sliced green onions, both green and white parts, for garnish

2 tablespoons roasted black and white sesame seeds, for garnish

Soba Noodles
Soba

Serves 6

Soba are one of the Japanese signature noodles, and they are popular at soba-ya, noodle shops, along almost every street in Japan. Buckwheat flour is mixed with wheat flour, for its elasticity, and then made into soba noodles. Other ingredients may be added to create variations, such as green tea powder to make cha soba, green tea soba. Fresh soba noodles are the most desirable, but they are hard to find outside Japan. Serve this soup with two or three pieces of Tempura (page 90) on the side. For a spicy touch, sprinkle some Japanese chile mix (ichimi or shichimi togarashi) over the noodles.

To make the seaweed broth, wipe the kelp clean with damp paper towels. Combine the water and kelp in a pot and let stand for 30 minutes.

Bring to just a simmer over medium heat (do not bring to a rolling boil). Simmer for 10 to 12 minutes. Remove the kelp using a wire strainer or tongs and discard. Stir the vegetable base into the broth.

To make the soup broth, put all the ingredients in a medium pot and bring to a boil. Decrease the heat to low to keep the broth warm.

Seaweed Broth
Dashi

2 to 3 pieces (3 to 4 ounces) dried kelp (*dashi kombu*)

8 cups water

1 tablespoon vegetable or seaweed base (flavor enhancer or bouillon cube)

Soup Broth

6 to 7 cups Seaweed Broth (see recipe above)

3/4 cup mirin (cooking sake)

1/2 cup soy sauce, or more to taste

2 tablespoons sugar

1 teaspoon salt

To cook the noodles, put 8 cups of water in a pot and bring to a boil. Add the noodles and stir frequently to keep them from sticking together. When the water returns to a boil, pour in about $1/3$ cup of cold water to lower the temperature. Repeat the process when the water boils again. Test the noodles; they should be slightly softer than al dente. (Repeat the process, if necessary.) Drain the noodles in a sieve and rinse thoroughly with cold water (use your fingers to comb the noodles), until they are free of sticky starch.

To serve, heat the soup broth to almost boiling. Warm the noodles with hot water (dip the noodles in boiling water or rinse them with hot water), and then divide them among individual serving bowls. Sprinkle the noodles with the mushrooms.

Pour the hot soup broth over the noodles. Garnish with the green onions. Serve immediately. Pass the bottle of *ichimi togarashi* at the table, if desired.

Noodles and Condiments

4 to 5 ounces dried soba noodles, or 8 to 10 ounces fresh soba noodles

2 cups very thinly sliced shiitake mushrooms or mushrooms of your choice

2 stalks green onions, both green and white parts thinly sliced on the diagonal

1 bottle *ichimi* or *shichimi togarashi* (Japanese chile mix; optional)

Spicy Tofu
Takanotsume Dofu

Serves 6

Spicy food found its way into Japanese cuisine when chiles were introduced in the sixteenth century. Dried chiles are popular in Japanese food; they are processed into powder, ready-made chile sauce, mixed spices, and hot oil. This spicy tofu dish can be served as a filling for sushi rolls, a topping for rice bowls, a dip for chips and vegetables, or a side dish or condiment to add spiciness to any meal. It is very easy to make, but you will need to have all the chile condiments on hand. Japanese chile condiments come in small, brightly colored bottles; they store very well and will keep a long time in the pantry.

1 pound (2 cups) firm silken tofu, well drained and crumbled

⅓ cup soy mayonnaise (optional)

1 tablespoon soy sauce, or more to taste

1 tablespoon sesame chile oil (*ra-yu*)

1 tablespoon mirin (cooking sake)

2 teaspoons chile paste (*shisen toban jan* or *sambal oelek*)

1 teaspoon *ichimi* or *shichimi togarashi* (Japanese dried chile mix)

P ut all the ingredients in a mixing bowl. Mix until well combined.

Sushi Rice
Su-Meshi

Makes 6 to 7 cups; serves 6

Sushi rice recipes will not always work perfectly on the first try. Cooking rice over a gas stove or with an electric rice cooker will result in different outcomes. Most sushi chefs recommend using a rice cooker so that the texture of the rice is consistent. Sushi rice recipes should be viewed as a general guide; adjustments will need to be made to fit each particular circumstance.

3 cups Japanese sushi rice

3 cups cold water, plus or minus $1/4$ cup

$1/3$ cup rice vinegar

2 tablespoons sugar

1 teaspoon salt

Place the rice in a medium bowl and fill the bowl with cold water to about 2 inches above the rice. Wash the rice with both hands by rubbing the grains gently together. Drain. Repeat the rubbing process 2 to 3 times, with fresh water each time, until the water is almost clear. Drain in a colander.

Combine the rice with the 3 cups (plus or minus $1/4$ cup) cold water in a pot over medium-high heat. (Add enough water to cover the rice and so that the water comes up to the first knuckle on your index finger if you're touching the rice with the tip of your finger.) Stir to mix well.

Bring the water and rice to a boil. Decrease the heat to medium-low, cover with a lid, and cook for 15 to 20 minutes, or until all the liquid has been absorbed. Turn off the heat and let the pot stand on hot stove for 7 to 10 minutes. It is very important to not lift the lid during this standing period; the rice will continue to steam, even though the heat is off.

To make the dressing, combine the vinegar, sugar, and salt in a pot over medium heat. Cook and stir until the sugar and salt are dissolved. Remove from the heat.

To make the sushi rice, transfer the cooked rice to a large, nonreactive bowl (such as one made from glass, ceramic, or wood). Slowly sprinkle the vinegar mixture over the rice while folding and mixing the rice with a wet wooden spoon or spatula. Take care not to cut the grains as you mix or the rice will become mushy. (A simple tip to make the perfect sushi rice is to get rid of moisture quickly by mixing the rice in moving air, such as near a fan or open window.) Do not overwork the rice or its texture will be ruined.

Sushi rice is best used immediately. If you cannot use it immediately, keep the rice at room temperature, covered with a damp towel to prevent it from drying out, and use it is soon as possible.

Tempura

Tempura

Serves 6

Deep-frying is a cooking technique that is popular throughout Asia, as it provides a crispy, crunchy texture and brightens flavors. The technique for Japanese tempura was acquired from Portuguese traders in the seventeenth century. The keys to successful tempura are using fresh cooking oil and maintaining the proper temperature so the ingredients taste clean and bright and the batter fries to the perfect crispness without absorbing too much oil. For convenience, use premade tempura powder, which is readily available in a paper box at Asian markets. It is a mixture of a variety of flours, seasonings, and spices.

3 cups vegetable oil, for deep-frying

$3/4$ cup ice-cold water

$1/2$ cup ice cubes

1 cup tempura powder, plus more as needed

$1/4$ teaspoon salt

18 sticks (each stick 3 x $1/4$ inch) peeled kabocha squash and/or sweet potato

18 sticks (each stick 3 x $1/4$ inch) carrots

18 broccoli and/or cauliflower florets

18 green beans and/or green pea pods, trimmed

18 pieces peeled and thinly sliced lotus roots

1 bottle tempura sauce or soy sauce

Heat the oil in a deep pan to between 350 and 375 degrees F.

Mix the water with the ice in a medium mixing bowl. Gradually add the tempura powder and salt, stirring briefly with a pair of chopsticks. The batter should be fairly lumpy. Test and taste the batter by first frying just one piece of one of the vegetables. The batter should adhere to the vegetables. If it does not, the batter is too thin, and you will need to add more powder as necessary. Add more salt to taste.

Dip the vegetables into the batter and then lower them into the pan to fit loosely. Deep-fry the vegetables for 3 to 5 minutes, turning them occasionally, until they are crispy and golden brown all over. Drain on a rack or on absorbent paper.

Serve hot with tempura sauce on the side.

Yakitori

Yakitori

Serves 6

This dish serves as a light snack or nibble to accompany drinks, such as tea or sake. There are millions of small shops, known as yakitori bars, throughout Japan, established for the sole purpose of serving drinks and snacks, called tsumami. *Yakitori dishes made with yakitori sauce are very popular items on the menus.*

Slice the eggplants and mushrooms into strips about 1½ inches long and 1 inch thick.

Using only the firm white and green parts of the green onions, cut them into ³/₄-inch-long sticks.

Thread the eggplant strips on the bamboo skewers, with a piece of green onion in between each strip. Leave about 1 inch at the end of each stick for a handle. Thread the mushroom strips on the bamboo skewers the same way. Set aside.

Combine the soy sauce, optional ginger, mirin, sake, sugar, sesame oil, salt, and pepper in a small pot over medium-low heat. Simmer for 10 to 12 minutes, until the mixture becomes a thin sauce.

Pour half of the soy sauce mixture in a bowl and set aside. Pour the remaining soy sauce mixture into a shallow tray. Arrange the skewered vegetables in the tray and turn them so the sauce coats them evenly. Let marinate for 15 to 20 minutes, turning occasionally, until the grill is ready.

½ pound Asian long purple eggplants
½ pound portobello mushrooms
1 bunch green onions
1 package bamboo skewers (6 inches long), soaked in water for 30 minutes
½ cup soy sauce
¼ cup peeled and matchstick-sliced ginger (optional)
¼ cup mirin (cooking sake)
¼ cup sake
2 tablespoons sugar
½ teaspoon sesame oil
½ teaspoon salt
½ teaspoon ground pepper
Vegetable oil, for grilling
2 tablespoons roasted black and white sesame seeds, for garnish
1 lemon, cut into 6 wedges

Start a charcoal grill, broiler, or grill pan to obtain a medium heat. Apply a light coating of oil to the grill or pan and cook the eggplants and mushrooms until tender (5 to 6 minutes for the eggplants and 3 to 4 minutes for the mushrooms), turning them several times and brushing them with more of the soy sauce mixture.

Transfer to a serving plate and sprinkle with the sesame seeds. Serve hot, with the reserved sauce and the lemon wedges.

Korea

Pickled Vegetables
Kimchi

Makes 4 to 5 cups; serves 6

Kimchi is often on the tip of the tongue whenever Korean food is discussed. Its strong aroma and intense flavor have given it a prominent place as a side dish with Korean meals. It is very easy to make but takes a long time to cure. As with all pickled foods, cleanliness is essential in order to avoid mold during the long fermentation period. A variety of popular pickling vegetables are suitable for this dish, such as cabbage, carrots, cucumbers, and daikon, but cabbage is the most preferred because of its concentrated flavor. If you find the smell of fermented cabbage bothersome, select your favorite vegetables instead or try fresh kimchi without fermenting.

2 pounds napa cabbage, Chinese cabbage, or vegetable of your choice

1$^{1}/_{2}$ to 2 tablespoons sea salt or regular table salt

$^{1}/_{2}$ to 1 cup (1 ounce) dried small chiles, more or less to taste

1 cup chopped green onions, green part only

$^{1}/_{4}$ cup chopped garlic

2 tablespoons peeled and chopped fresh ginger (optional)

1 tablespoon sugar, more or less to taste

Separate and clean the cabbage thoroughly with cold water. Drain in a colander. Break the cabbage coarsely with your hands or slice it with a clean knife into small pieces. Return the cabbage to the colander, sprinkle with the salt, and mix thoroughly. Let the cabbage stand for at least 1 hour. Thoroughly rinse the cabbage under cold running water. Set aside to drain completely.

Coarsely break the chiles or cut them into small pieces. Soak in warm water for 10 to 15 minutes, until soft. Drain well.

Combine the cabbage, chiles, green onions, garlic, optional ginger, and sugar in a large, clean mixing bowl. Mix and toss thoroughly until well combined. Stuff the mixture into an airtight jar or container, seal tightly, and let cure in a cool dark place for 3 to 4 days. After being cured, the kimchi can be used immediately or refrigerated for up to 4 weeks.

Fresh Kimchi: Use the same ingredients and directions for the standard recipe but add 2 tablespoons light soy sauce, 2 tablespoons chopped fresh cilantro leaves, and 1 tablespoon chopped fresh red chiles. Combine all the ingredients in a clean mixing bowl. Serve immediately.

Steamed Vegetable Rolls

Twaejigogi Saekchim

Serves 6

Although this dish sounds complicated, its preparation and cooking methods are very straightforward. Korean food, with influences from China and Japan, often uses stuffing in food preparation and steaming for the cooking technique. This recipe uses both popular techniques in this delicious dish, which can be served as a soup or a full meal with steamed rice.

6 to 8 dried shiitake or black mushrooms
4 cups vegetable stock
6 to 8 large napa cabbage leaves, washed
$1^{1}/2$ cups thinly sliced button mushrooms
$1^{1}/2$ cups matchstick-sliced carrots
$1^{1}/2$ cups matchstick-sliced zucchini
$1/2$ cup roasted pine nuts, plus more for garnish
2 tablespoons minced garlic
2 tablespoons peeled and minced fresh ginger
2 tablespoons light soy sauce
1 tablespoon fermented bean curds (optional)
1 tablespoon mirin (cooking sake)
1 tablespoon vegetable base (flavor enhancer or bouillon cube)
1 teaspoon sesame oil
$1/2$ teaspoon ground pepper
1 lemon, cut into 6 wedges

Soak the dried mushrooms in warm water for 15 to 20 minutes, until soft. Drain and squeeze out the excess water. Trim and discard the stems and thinly slice the caps.

Bring the vegetable stock to a boil in a pot over medium heat. Briefly blanch the napa cabbage leaves for 1 to 2 minutes, until soft and pliable. Remove from the pot and spread out on a flat surface. If ridges in the middle of the leaves are too thick and not pliable, preventing them from being rolled, use a sharp knife to slice and flatten the ridges to make them thinner and more pliable. If the leaves are too big, cut them in half lengthwise. Reserve the vegetable stock.

Scatter both kinds of mushrooms and the carrots, zucchini, and pine nuts over the cabbage leaves, covering about three-quarters of each leaf but keeping about a $1/2$-inch margin around the edges. Sprinkle with a little salt and pepper. Fold the edges of the leaf to cover the filling and roll the leaf to wrap the filling tightly into a log. Repeat the process with all the cabbage leaves. Place the rolls in heatproof bowls (with 1 or 2 rolls per bowl) or arrange them all on a large dish. Place the bowls or dish on a steamer tray. Set aside.

Add the garlic, ginger, soy sauce, optional fermented bean curds, mirin, vegetable base, sesame oil, and pepper to the vegetable stock. Adjust the seasonings to taste. Stir to mix well. Distribute the stock into the bowls or the dish of rolled vegetables. Place the steamer over high heat and steam the rolls for 8 to 10 minutes, until all the vegetables are tender and cooked through.

Serve the hot rolls in bowls, garnished with additional pine nuts. Serve the lemon wedges and additional seasonings of your choice on the side.

Steamed Stuffed Eggplants
Kajitchim

Serves 6

Asian eggplants come in many varieties: small marble sized to large baseball sized, short and stumpy to long and slender, pale yellow and green to dark purple, tangy bitter to sweet nutty, and soft and spongy to firm and crunchy. The cooking time needs to be taken into consideration, depending on the types and sizes of eggplants used in this recipe: for firm, dense varieties, increase the cooking time; for soft, spongy varieties, decrease the cooking time.

To make stuffing, heat the vegetable and sesame oils in a wok over medium heat. Stir in the shallots, garlic, chiles, ginger, and sesame seeds. Cook and stir for 2 to 3 minutes, until the shallots and garlic are light brown and fragrant.

Stir in both kinds of mushrooms and the soy sauce, sugar, and vegetable base. Cook and stir for 2 to 3 minutes, until the mushrooms are tender. Stir in the tofu, green onions, and parsley. Cook and stir for 2 to 3 minutes, until all the ingredients are heated through. Adjust the seasonings to taste. Set aside.

Stuffing

3 tablespoons vegetable oil

1 teaspoon sesame oil

3 tablespoons minced shallots

2 tablespoons minced garlic

2 tablespoons minced red chiles, more or less to taste

2 tablespoons peeled and minced fresh ginger

1 tablespoon sesame seeds

2 cups thinly sliced shiitake mushrooms

2 cups thinly sliced button mushrooms

2 tablespoons light soy sauce

2 tablespoons sugar

1 tablespoon vegetable base (flavor enhancer or bouillon cube)

1/2 pound silken tofu, well drained and crumbled

1/4 cup chopped green onions, both green and white parts

1/4 cup chopped fresh flat-leaf parsley

To prepare the stuffed eggplant, spread the chopped onions in a large pan with a lid or in a large baking or casserole dish and sprinkle with the salt. Pour the vegetable stock over the onions.

Use the eggplants whole, with the stems. Cut 4 lengthwise slits in each eggplant but don't cut all the way through, creating deep pockets along the eggplant with both ends intact. Arrange the eggplants in a single layer over the onions and spoon as much stuffing as will fit into each slit (pocket) of the eggplants.

Place the pan on the stove over medium-low heat and cover with the lid. Cook for 45 to 50 minutes, until the eggplant is tender. Check the liquid occasionally so the onions don't dry out and burn; add more stock or water, if necessary. Alternatively, preheat the oven to 350 degrees F and bake the eggplants in the covered pan for $1\frac{1}{2}$ hours.

Transfer the eggplants to a serving platter. Add the oil to the onions in the pan. Increase the heat to high and cook and stir the onions for 3 to 4 minutes, until brown. Spoon the onions over the eggplants. Serve warm.

Eggplants

3 cups chopped yellow onions

$\frac{1}{2}$ teaspoon salt

$\frac{1}{3}$ cup vegetable stock or water, plus more as needed

4 to 5 Asian long purple eggplants (1 pound)

2 tablespoons vegetable oil

Stir-Fried Vermicelli Noodles

Chapchae

This is a popular Korean noodle dish that can be served warm or at room temperature. A simple technique of stir-frying, borrowed from neighboring China, makes the dish easy and quick to prepare. All components of the dish can be made in advance and tossed together just before serving.

4 to 6 ounces dried rice vermicelli noodles

2 tablespoons light soy sauce, or more to taste

1 teaspoon sesame oil

2 tablespoons vegetable oil

2 tablespoons thinly sliced shallot

1 tablespoon chopped dried red chile, or more to taste

1 1/2 cups julienned carrots

1 1/2 cups julienned leeks

1 1/2 cups thinly sliced fresh shiitake mushrooms

2 tablespoons sugar, or more to taste

1 tablespoon vegetarian stir-fry sauce or seasoning soy sauce (such as Maggi Seasoning Sauce or mushroom-flavored soy sauce), or more to taste

1 tablespoon vegetable base (flavor enhancer or bouillon cube)

1/2 teaspoon ground pepper

1/4 pound baby spinach leaves, washed

2 tablespoons roasted sesame seeds, for garnish

Soak the noodles in warm water for 20 minutes, until soft and pliable. Refresh the water if necessary. Drain thoroughly in a colander.

Heat the soy sauce and sesame oil in a wok over medium heat. Add the noodles and cook and stir for 2 to 4 minutes to mix thoroughly. Taste and make sure that the noodles are cooked through. Transfer to a large bowl. Wipe the wok clean with paper towels.

Heat the vegetable oil in the wok. Add the shallot and chile and cook and stir for 1 to 2 minutes, until fragrant. Add the carrots, leeks, mushrooms, sugar, stir-fry sauce, vegetable base, and pepper. Cook and stir for 2 to 3 minutes, until the vegetables are tender.

Remove the wok from the heat. Add the noodles and toss to mix well. Adjust the seasonings to taste.

To serve, line a serving platter with the spinach and top with the noodles. Garnish with the sesame seeds before serving.

Laos

Braised Eggplant in Curry
Sousi

Serves 6

Laos and Thailand are close neighbors; the languages are so similar that their people can understand each other well. Their food also falls into the same category, as it includes similar ingredients and produces similar tastes and flavors. There is a subtle difference between the two cuisines, however, and only connoisseurs can tell them apart. This recipe, sousi, has a close cousin on the Thai menu called chuchee, which starts the same, with curry paste, coconut, and vegetables. But the Laotian sousi uses only fresh herbs to spice the curry while the Thai dish includes both fresh and dried spices. Serve it with steamed rice.

2 large, fresh red jalape-o or serrano chiles, seeded and chopped

3 tablespoons chopped lemongrass, tender midsection only

3 tablespoons chopped shallots

2 tablespoons chopped garlic

2 tablespoons chopped Thai red chiles (for more spicy heat; optional)

2 tablespoons chopped fresh cilantro

2 tablespoons chopped fresh dill

1 tablespoon peeled and chopped galangal

1 tablespoon chopped kaffir lime skin (zest) or fresh kaffir lime leaves

1/2 cup coconut cream

1 pound Asian long purple eggplants, cut diagonally into 1/2-inch-thick pieces

1 cup coconut milk

3 to 4 whole fresh or dried kaffir lime leaves

2 tablespoons light soy sauce

1 tablespoon sugar

1 tablespoon vegetable base (flavor enhancer or bouillon cube)

1 cup whole Thai sweet basil leaves

Grind and pound the jalape-o chiles, lemongrass, shallots, garlic, Thai chiles, cilantro, dill, galangal, and kaffir lime skin into a smooth paste in a mortar with pestle. Alternatively, use a food processor, adding a small amount of coconut cream to facilitate processing.

Heat the coconut cream in a wok or deep pan over medium heat. Stir in the spice paste and cook and stir for 4 to 6 minutes, until fragrant. Stir in the eggplants and toss well so the paste coats them evenly.

Increase the heat to high and stir in the coconut milk, kaffir lime leaves, soy sauce, sugar, and vegetable base. Bring the mixture to a boil and continue cooking for 5 to 6 minutes, until the eggplants are tender and the liquid has reduced to a thick sauce.

Just before removing from the heat, stir in the basil leaves. Serve hot.

Caramelized Onions
Pad Som Hoam

Serves 6

This recipe emphasizes the sweet-and-spicy flavor of Asian small red onions, which are similar to shallots but sweeter and rounder in shape. Caramelizing onions makes their flavor more intense and adds a touch of smoky aroma. To get a sweet-and-tangy flavor, use ready-made pickled onions in a jar. Serve this dish hot, with steamed rice.

To make the carmelized onions, combine all the ingredients in a pan over high heat. Bring to a boil. Decrease the heat to low and simmer for 7 to 8 minutes, stirring occasionally, until the liquid has evaporated and the onions are caramelized. Set aside.

To make the tofu and coconut, heat the oil in another pan or a wok over medium heat. Add the garlic and cook and stir for 1 to 2 minutes, until light brown and fragrant. Stir in the tofu, coconut cream, soy sauce, vegetable base, and pepper. Bring to a boil and continue cooking for 7 to 8 minutes, until the liquid is reduced by half and the sauce thickens.

Just before serving, stir in the green onions, cilantro, and caramelized onions. Adjust the seasonings and add more lime juice to taste. Serve hot.

Caramelized Onions

1 pound Asian small red onions, peeled pearl onions, or pickled pearl onions in a jar

1/4 cup freshly squeezed lime juice, or more to taste

1/4 cup water

2 tablespoons sugar

1 teaspoon salt

Tofu and Coconut

2 tablespoons vegetable oil

3 tablespoons chopped garlic

1 1/2 pounds pressed or firm tofu, diced

1 3/4 cups coconut cream (one 14-ounce can)

2 tablespoons light soy sauce

1 tablespoon vegetable base (flavor enhancer or bouillon cube)

1/2 teaspoon ground pepper

1/4 cup thinly sliced green onions, green part only

1/4 cup chopped fresh cilantro leaves

Green Papaya Salad
Tom Som

Serves 6

This is an all-time popular salad and snack in many Southeast Asian countries: Cambodia, Thailand, Vietnam, and Laos each has its own delicious version. Recently, the traditional recipe has been modified and embellished, taking it to new heights and diversifying both the taste and texture. Fresh vegetables and fruits of your choice (especially those marked as optional in the ingredient list) can be added, as most will pair well with the near-neutral taste and very crunchy texture of the green papaya. Fragrant leaves, such as kaffir lime leaves, sawtooth herb, and Thai sweet basil provide another dimension and distinguish this Laotian salad from other cuisines. Locals serve this intensely flavored salad with a lot of fresh salad leaves and rice noodles, called kanom sen.

½ pound green papaya

1 cup matchstick-sliced carrot

1 cup peeled and thinly sliced jicama (optional)

1 cup seeded and thinly sliced cucumber (optional)

1 cup thinly sliced cabbage (optional)

1 cup thinly sliced green mango (optional)

1 cup thinly slice banana blossoms (optional)

1 cup sliced Asian long beans or green beans, cut into 1-inch-long strips

3 tablespoons minced garlic, or more to taste

2 tablespoons minced Thai chiles, more or less to taste

1 cup seeded and diced tomatoes

1 cup chopped fresh cilantro leaves

½ cup chopped roasted peanuts and/or cashew nuts or other nuts (such as macadamia or pistachio)

¼ cup very thinly sliced (chiffonade) fresh kaffir lime leaves

¼ cup very thinly sliced (chiffonade) fresh mint or Vietnamese mint leaves (optional)

¼ cup very thinly sliced (chiffonade) fresh sawtooth herb (optional)

Peel the papaya, removing the green skin completely. Rinse with cold water and cut it in half lengthwise. Discard the seeds. With a knife, mandoline, or hand shredder, slice the pale greenish white flesh into fine matchsticks. Do the same with the carrot and optional vegetables and fruits and arrange them separately into piles of matchsticks on a tray.

Using a mortar with pestle or a stainless steel bowl with a rolling pin, lightly grind and pound the long beans, garlic, and chiles to mix them well and lightly break up the long beans. Add the papaya, carrot, and optional vegetables or fruits of your choice. With a long spoon, stir and turn the ingredients with one hand and lightly pound with the pestle in the other hand.

dd the tomatoes, cilantro, peanuts, kaffir lime leaves, optional fresh herbs of your choice, lime juice, soy sauce, sugar, and optional fermented bean curds. Adjust the seasonings and ingredients to taste. Stir and lightly pound until all the ingredients are thoroughly mixed.

Transfer to a serving platter. Serve with the lettuce and optional rice noodles.

1/4 cup very thinly sliced (chiffonade) fresh Thai sweet basil leaves (optional)

3 tablespoons freshly squeezed lime juice, or more to taste

2 tablespoons light soy sauce, or more to taste

2 tablespoons sugar, or more to taste

1 tablespoon fermented bean curds (optional)

1 head lettuce, washed and separated into leaves (for wrappers)

1/2 pound dried rice noodles, cooked according to the package instructions (optional)

1 cup fresh Vietnamese mint leaves

1 cup fresh mint leaves

Eggplant Dip
Tom Ponh

Serves 6

This is a truly healthful and tasty dip that is popular at many Laotian meals. Its concentrated flavor requires many fresh leafy greens and herbs as accompaniments to help dilute the intensity; of course, this promotes eating more vegetables.

To make the dip, cook the whole eggplants over medium heat on a grill or bake them in an oven at 375 degrees F for 10 to 12 minutes, until soft and cooked through. (For a shortcut, cook the eggplants in a microwave until soft and cooked through.) Let cool. Cut each eggplant in half lengthwise. With a spoon, scoop out the flesh and set side.

Wrap the garlic, shallots, and both kinds of chiles in a piece of aluminum foil in the shape of a flat envelope. Place the envelope on the grill or on top of the stove over medium heat. Roast, turning occasionally, for 3 to 4 minutes, until fragrant. Set aside to cool.

Combine the eggplant flesh and roasted garlic mixture in a food processor. Add the green onions, lime juice, mint leaves, cilantro leaves, dill, soy sauce, optional fermented bean curds, sugar, vegetable base, and salt. Pulse until well combined, adding a little water if the texture is too thick. Adjust the seasonings to taste. Transfer to a bowl.

Arrange all the accompaniments around the bowl of eggplant dip on a serving platter. For self-service, take a leaf wrapper and fill it with herbs and vegetables. Spoon a dollop of the eggplant dip on top, roll up the leaf, and eat it with your hands.

Dip

1 pound Asian long purple eggplants

3 tablespoons chopped garlic

3 tablespoons chopped shallots

3 tablespoons chopped green jalape–o or serrano chiles

2 tablespoons chopped Thai chiles, more or less to taste

1/4 cup chopped green onions, both green and white parts

1/4 cup freshly squeezed lime juice, or more to taste

3 tablespoons chopped fresh mint leaves

3 tablespoons chopped fresh cilantro leaves

3 tablespoons chopped fresh dill

2 tablespoons light soy sauce, or more to taste

2 tablespoons fermented bean curds (optional)

1 tablespoon sugar

1 tablespoon vegetable base (flavor enhancer or bouillon cube)

1/4 teaspoon salt, or more to taste

Accompaniments

1 head lettuce, washed, trimmed, and separated into leaves (for wrappers)

2 cups thinly sliced hothouse cucumber, cut into half-moons

2 cups vegetables of your choice

1 cup fresh Thai sweet basil leaves

1 cup fresh cilantro leaves

Malaysia

Dry Curry
Kambing Rendang

Serves 6

This is a dish with Indian influences and Malaysian sensibility. Curry originated in India and was passed along through Asia. When it arrived in Southeast Asia, the locals added native spices to it, and curry became almost a way of life. This recipe uses a method of slow cooking so the flavor seeps through all the ingredients. The potatoes should be cooked just until almost tender so they don't disintegrate and turn this dry curry into a soup. Serve this dish hot with steamed rice or flat breads.

To make the spice paste, stem, seed, and soak the chiles in warm water for 10 to 15 minutes, until soft. Drain and squeeze dry.

Combine the cloves, coriander, cumin, and fennel seeds in a small, dry pan over medium heat. Roast, shaking the pan occasionally, for 3 to 4 minutes, until the seeds are fragrant and starting to crackle and pop. Let cool.

Grind and pound the roasted spices into a powder in a mortar with pestle. Add the remaining ingredients, one at a time, and pound until the mixture turns into a smooth paste. Alternatively, combine all the ingredients in a food processor and process into a smooth paste, adding a little water to facilitate processing.

Spice Paste

3 to 4 large dried red chiles (Mexican, guajillo, puya, or California)

6 whole cloves

2 tablespoons whole coriander seeds

1 tablespoon whole cumin seeds

1 teaspoon whole fennel seeds

3 tablespoons chopped lemongrass, tender midsection only

3 tablespoons chopped shallots

2 tablespoons chopped garlic

2 tablespoons peeled and chopped fresh ginger

1 teaspoon salt

1/2 teaspoon ground nutmeg

1/2 teaspoon ground turmeric

To make the curry, put the oil in a pot over medium heat. Stir in the spice paste and cook for 3 to 4 minutes, until fragrant. Stir in the potatoes, vegetable stock, and cinnamon stick. Cook, stirring occasionally, for 7 to 8 minutes, until the potatoes are almost tender.

Stir in the tofu, coconut cream, tamarind liquid, coconut flakes, soy sauce, sugar, and vegetable base. Bring to a boil, stirring gently but constantly, until the liquid has evaporated into a thick sauce that evenly coats the potatoes and tofu. Adjust the seasonings to taste.

Transfer to a serving platter and garnish with the cucumber. Serve hot.

Curry

2 tablespoons vegetable oil

1 pound potatoes, peeled and diced

2 cups vegetable stock

1 cinnamon stick

1 pound fried tofu, diced

1 cup coconut cream

1/3 cup tamarind liquid

1/4 cup dried unsweetened coconut flakes

2 tablespoons light soy sauce

2 tablespoons palm or brown sugar, or more to taste

1 tablespoon vegetable base (flavor enhancer or bouillon cube)

1 hothouse cucumber, cut in half lengthwise and thinly sliced into half-moons, for garnish

Celebratory Golden Rice
Nasi Kunyit

Serves 6

Malaysian people celebrate their large and small events with food, and nasi kunyit *is at the center of it. This mound of golden rice is the staple; it's the starch that accompanies a variety of large and small dishes of both food and condiments. For celebrations, a wide range of foods with a diversity of ingredients, tastes, textures, colors, and methods of cooking are assembled. The greater the assortment, the more elevated the status of the host. The mound of yellow rice is often decorated with colorful, edible fruits and vegetables, shaped and carved to represent gemstones that stud the golden mountain.*

To cook the rice more quickly, soak it for 3 to 12 hours and drain. If using a rice cooker, combine all the ingredients in the cooker, stir to mix well, and turn the machine on according to the manufacturer's instructions.

If cooking on the stove, combine all the ingredients in a pot and bring to a boil. Decrease the heat to low, cover with a tight-fitting lid, and cook for 12 to 15 minutes, until the liquid is all absorbed and the rice is tender. Turn the heat off and let the pot rest on the hot stove for an additional 5 to 7 minutes.

To serve, place the banana leaf on a serving platter. Mound the rice on the banana leaf and discard the pandan leaves.

2 cups long-grain sweet rice or glutinous rice

1³/4 cups (one 14-ounce can) coconut milk or cream

1 cup vegetable stock or water

1 to 2 stalks lemongrass, cut into 2-inch-long sticks and crushed to break open

2 whole dried pandan leaves, kaffir lime leaves, or bay leaves

1 tablespoon sugar, more or less to taste

1 tablespoon vegetable base (flavor enhancer or bouillon cube)

1 teaspoon ground turmeric

1 teaspoon salt

1 piece banana leaf or Hawaiian ti leaves, for serving the rice (optional)

Mushrooms in Tamarind Sauce
Goreng Asam

Serves 6

This recipe requires ingredients with good absorption properties, such as mushrooms and eggplants, to lock in the sweet-and-sour tamarind flavor. Ready-made tamarind liquid or concentrate is available in a jar in the dry goods section of Asian grocery stores. Tamarind pulp in a square block wrapped in plastic is also available. To get the tamarind liquid from the pulp, simply soak a small chunk of pulp in a little hot water and squeeze and strain out the brown liquid.

1/2 pound abalone or portabella mushrooms (select large, thick mushrooms)

1/2 pound Asian long purple eggplants

1 cup tamarind liquid, plus more as needed

3 tablespoons vegetable oil, plus more as needed

1 teaspoon salt, or more to taste

1 tablespoon sugar

1 cup sliced green onions, both green and white parts, cut into 1-inch-long strips

1 tablespoon minced garlic (optional)

1 tablespoon minced red chiles (optional)

1/2 teaspoon ground pepper, for garnish

Slice the mushrooms into several long pieces, each about 1/2 inch thick. Slice the eggplant diagonally into several pieces, each about 1/2 inch thick. Combine the mushrooms, eggplants, and tamarind liquid in a bowl. Gently toss to combine well. Let stand for 10 to 15 minutes. Remove the vegetables from the tamarind liquid just before you are ready to cook them. Reserve the remaining tamarind liquid, if there is any left.

Heat some of the oil in a large pan or wok over medium-high heat. Tilt the pan and swirl the oil to coat the pan's surface. Sprinkle some of the salt over the oil. When the oil is hot and lightly smoking, add the mushrooms and eggplants to fit the pan in a single layer. Cook for 1 to 2 minutes, until the bottoms of the vegetables are brown. Turn the vegetables over and cook the other side until browned and cooked through. Remove from the pan and keep warm. Add more oil and salt and cook the remaining vegetables the same way.

Combine the remaining tamarind liquid (adding more as needed to make a glaze) and the sugar in the same pan. Cook and stir for 1 to 2 minutes, until the mixture turns into a glaze. Return the mushrooms and eggplants to the pan. Stir in the green onions and optional garlic and chiles. Gently stir and toss to mix well.

Transfer to a serving platter and sprinkle with the pepper. Serve hot.

Baked Spiced Mousse
Otak Otak

Serves 6; makes 12 pieces

This is a fun recipe to put together that boasts a tropical and exotic touch. Banana leaves are versatile and serve many purposes in Malaysia, from roof thatching to food wrapping. Utensils, such as plates, bowls, cups, and doilies, can be made from banana leaves. Not only do the leaves gift a sweet fragrance to the food, they are also biodegradable and need no cleaning, which saves water, soap, and time.

To make the spice paste, stem, seed, and soak the dried chiles in warm water for 10 to 15 minutes, until soft. Drain and squeeze dry.

Grind and pound the dried chiles in a mortar with pestle. Add the remaining ingredients, one at a time, and pound until the mixture turns into a smooth paste. Alternatively, combine all the ingredients in a food processor and process into a smooth paste, adding a small amount of water to facilitate processing.

Spice Paste

3 to 4 dried large red chiles (Mexican, guajillo, puya, or California)

2 fresh red Thai chiles, more or less to taste

3 tablespoons chopped shallots

2 tablespoons chopped garlic

2 tablespoons chopped lemongrass, tender midsection only

2 tablespoons chopped roasted peanuts, candlenuts, or almonds

1 tablespoon peeled and chopped fresh ginger

1 teaspoon ground turmeric

1 teaspoon salt

To make the mousse, combine the spice paste (page 110), tofu, coconut cream, kaffir lime leaves, soy sauce, sugar, vegetable base, and salt in a food processor. Pulse several times until well combined. Do not overprocess or the mixture will separate.

If the banana leaves are too stiff and break easily when folding, roast them briefly on a hot stove or over open flame. To wrap, stack two banana leaves to make a wrapper and arrange them in a diamond shape facing you. Scoop about 3 tablespoons of the mousse into the middle of the wrapper and form a thin, 2 x 5-inch rectangular cake. Sprinkle with a few strips of the red chiles. Pull together the bottom and top points over the cake, fold them tightly and snuggly on top of the cake. Fold in both side points and secure each point with a toothpick to make a packet. Repeat the wrapping to use up all the mousse.

To cook, prepare a charcoal grill or a grill pan in advance to obtain medium heat. Grill the packets for 2 to 3 minutes on each side, until cooked through.

Transfer to a platter. Serve hot or at room temperature.

Mousse

1 pound firm silken tofu, well drained

¹/₂ cup coconut cream

3 tablespoons very thinly sliced (chiffonade) fresh kaffir lime leaves

2 tablespoons light soy sauce

2 tablespoons granulated sugar, or more to taste

1 tablespoon vegetable base (flavor enhancer or bouillon cube)

¹/₂ teaspoon salt

1 package banana leaves, cut into 24 pieces, each about 8 to 10 inches square (for wrappers)

1 cup matchstick-sliced red chiles or red bell pepper, for garnish

Spicy Grilled Eggplants
Sambal Brinjal

Serves 6

This dish is from nyonya descendants, people who are a mixture of native Malay and Chinese settlers. The distinction between native Malay and Chinese ingredients in their dishes is obvious. Nyonya also use a mortar with pestle to grind and pound their curry pastes, and using this tool is an art in itself that was handed down from prior generations, along with secret recipes that are family heirlooms.

6 Asian long purple long eggplants (1 to 1½ pounds)

2 tablespoons vegetable oil, plus more as needed

3 tablespoons chopped shallots

2 tablespoons chopped garlic

2 tablespoons chopped Thai or jalape–o chiles, more or less to taste

2 tablespoons chopped lemongrass, tender midsection only (optional)

1 tablespoon chopped kaffir lime skin (zest) or fresh kaffir lime leaves (optional)

2 tablespoons vegetable oil

2 tablespoons fermented bean curds (optional)

2 tablespoons light soy sauce

1 tablespoon sugar

1 tablespoon vinegar or freshly squeezed lemon juice

Heat a charcoal grill in advance. Cut the eggplants in half lengthwise and brush them thoroughly with oil. Grill the eggplants for 3 to 5 minutes on each side, until cooked and charred brown (but not burnt) all over. Remove from the grill and keep warm. Alternatively, instead of grilling, roast the eggplants in the oven at 375 degrees F for 10 to 15 minutes, until cooked through and browned.

Grind and pound the shallots, garlic, chiles, and the optional lemongrass and kaffir lime skin into a paste in a mortar with pestle. Alternatively, process them into a paste in a food processor.

To make the sauce, heat the oil in a pan over medium heat. Stir in the shallot paste and cook for 2 to 3 minutes, until light brown and fragrant. Stir in the optional fermented bean curds, soy sauce, sugar, and vinegar. Cook and stir for 2 to 3 minutes, until the mixture turns golden brown. Add a small amount of water if the mixture is too dry.

To serve, arrange the eggplants cut-side up on a serving plate. Spread the sauce over the eggplants. Serve warm or at room temperature.

Filipino Hot-and-Sour Soup
(Sinigang Na Hipon), page 120

Malaysian Spicy Okra
(Sambal Bhindi), p. 114

Spicy Fruit Salad
Rojak

Serves 6

Seasonal fruits and vegetables are suitable for this salad, so take advantage of the season's best tastes, textures, and prices. This is by no means a light salad. The dressing is full of zip and kicks, which turn ordinary fruits and vegetables into a vortex of heightened taste.

Bring a large pot of water to a full boil. Blanch the morning glory for 1 to 2 minutes, until tender. Remove from the pot with a wire skimmer and rinse under cold water until cool. Set aside in a colander to drip dry.

In the same boiling water, blanch the bean sprouts for under 1 minute, and then rinse them with cold water until cool. Set aside.

To make the salad dressing, combine the chiles, lime juice, tamarind liquid, optional fermented bean curds, soy sauce, sugar, and salt in a bowl. Stir to mix well, until the sugar is dissolved. Adjust the seasonings to taste.

Arrange the tofu, vegetables, and fruits on a serving platter. Just before serving, sprinkle with the dressing and toss gently to coarsely mix. Garnish with the peanuts. Serve at room temperature.

$1/4$ pound Asian morning glory or spinach, washed and trimmed

$1/4$ pound bean sprouts

3 large, red jalape–o or serrano chiles, seeded and minced

$1/4$ cup freshly squeezed lime or lemon juice

$1/4$ cup tamarind liquid or paste

2 tablespoons fermented bean curds (optional)

2 tablespoons light soy sauce

2 tablespoons palm or brown sugar

$1/4$ teaspoon salt

$1/4$ pound fried tofu, cut into $1/2$-inch squares

1 cup peeled and matchstick-sliced jicama

1 cup peeled and matchstick-sliced green mango

1 cup finely diced hothouse cucumber

1 cup finely diced pineapple

1 star fruit, cut into bite-sized pieces

$1/3$ cup roasted peanuts, coarsely chopped

Spicy Okra
Sambal Bhindi

Serves 6

See photo facing page 113.

Small, young okra pods are well suited for this dish, as they will mix best with the homemade sambal (chile paste). It is quite easy and quick to make, and pickled garlic or vinegar-seasoned garlic is a must for an authentic touch.

3 tablespoons vegetable oil

¼ cup minced shallots

2 tablespoons minced garlic

2 red jalape–o or serrano chiles, seeded and minced

1 pound young okra, trimmed and cut diagonally into 1-inch-long pieces

1 cup julienned firm or pressed tofu

1 cup julienned colorful bell peppers

¼ cup tamarind liquid or paste

2 tablespoons light soy sauce

2 tablespoons fermented bean curds (optional)

1 tablespoon sugar, or more to taste

1 tablespoon vegetable base (flavor enhancer or bouillon cube)

1 head pickled garlic, peeled and chopped

Heat the oil in a wok over medium heat. Add the shallots, garlic, and chiles and cook and stir for 2 to 3 minutes, until fragrant.

Increase the heat to high and stir in the okra, tofu, and peppers. Cook for about 2 minutes, until tender. Add the tamarind liquid, soy sauce, optional fermented bean curds, sugar, and vegetable base. Cook and stir for 4 to 5 minutes, until well combined and cooked through.

Transfer to a serving platter and sprinkle with the pickled garlic.

Stir-Fried Yellow Noodles

Mee Goreng

Serves 6

With Chinese influence, Malaysians have incorporated all types of Chinese noodles into their cuisine. Hokkien, the native people of southern China, introduced yellow noodles to mee goreng, and Malaysians added local ingredients, making the dish to fit their own palate. Fresh yellow noodles are widely available at any Asian grocery store and are sought after for this dish. Dried noodles are also acceptable, but they must be presoaked.

Separate the fresh noodles so they are not clumped together. If using dried noodles, soak them in warm water for 15 to 20 minutes, until pliable, and then drain.

Heat the oil in a wok over medium-high heat. Cook and stir the shallots for 3 to 4 minutes, until light brown, fragrant, and crispy, taking care that they do not burn. Drain on absorbent paper. Set aside for garnish.

Using the same wok over medium-high heat, cook and stir the potato for 3 to 4 minutes, until partially done. Stir in the garlic and cook and stir for 2 to 3 minutes, until light brown and fragrant. Increase the heat to high and stir in the noodles, tofu, cabbage, and carrot. Cook and stir for 2 minutes, until well mixed and cooked through, making sure the noodles are not clumped together.

Sprinkle with the soy sauce, *kecap manis*, sugar, *sambal oelek*, tomato paste, and vegetable base. Toss to mix well. Cook until all the liquid has been absorbed and the noodles are cooked through. Taste the noodles for tenderness, adding some water if necessary. Adjust the seasonings to taste.

8 to 10 ounces fresh Hokkein yellow noodles, or 4 to 5 ounces dried Hokkein yellow noodles

1/4 cup vegetable oil

1/4 cup thinly sliced shallots

1 potato, peeled and finely diced

3 tablespoons chopped garlic

4 to 6 ounces fried tofu, julienned

1 cup matchstick-sliced cabbage

1 cup matchstick-sliced carrot

2 tablespoons light soy sauce

2 tablespoons *kecap manis* (Indonesian sweet soy sauce)

1 tablespoon sugar, or more to taste

1 tablespoon *sambal oelek* (Indonesian hot chile sauce)

1 tablespoon tomato paste

1 tablespoon vegetable base (flavor enhancer or bouillon cube)

4 ounces (2 cups) bean sprouts

1 cup seeded and finely diced tomato

2 stalks green onion, both green and white parts, cut into 1 1/2-inch-long strips

2 cups thinly sliced hothouse cucumber, cut into half-moons

1 lemon or lime, cut into 6 wedges

Just before removing from the heat, add the bean sprouts, tomato, and green onion. Stir and toss to combine well.

Transfer to a serving platter and garnish with the fried shallots. Serve the noodles hot, with the cucumber and lemon wedges on the side.

Philippines

Braised Vegetables with Peanut Sauce
Kari-Kari

Serves 6

Kari-kari is a classic, slow-cooked Filipino dish. As an island country, the Philippines have had many culinary influences, and their cuisine has become a conglomeration of tastes from China, India, Malaysia, Spain, and the Americas. For vegetarians, slow cooking, or braising, is limited by the cooking time of the chosen vegetables. Cooking the dish too long will cause the ingredients to disintegrate, which is not a desirable outcome, unless a soup is what you have in mind. Serve this kari-kari over hot rice.

6 to 8 large, dried black mushrooms, tough stems removed

1/3 cup long-grain white rice

1 teaspoon whole annatto seeds

3 tablespoons vegetable oil

2 cups chopped yellow onions

3 tablespoons chopped garlic

3 cups vegetable stock

1/2 cup finely chopped roasted peanuts

3 tablespoons light soy sauce

2 tablespoons sugar

1 tablespoon vegetable base (flavor enhancer or bouillon cube)

1/2 pound green beans, trimmed and cut into 1 1/2-inch-long sticks

1/2 pound Asian eggplants, cut in half lengthwise and sliced into thin half-moons

Soak the mushrooms in warm water for 10 to 15 minutes, or until soft. Drain and squeeze out the excess water.

Combine the rice and annatto seeds in a small, dry pan over medium heat. Roast, shaking the pan occasionally, for 7 to 10 minutes, or until the rice is light brown and fragrant. Remove from the pan and let cool. Process the mixture into a powder in a mortar with pestle or a spice grinder.

Heat the oil in a pot over medium heat. Add the onions and garlic and cook for 5 to 7 minutes, stirring occasionally, until light brown. Add the mushrooms, rice powder, vegetable stock, peanuts, soy sauce, sugar, and vegetable base, stirring to mix well. Bring to a boil, decrease the heat slightly, and simmer for 5 to 6 minutes, or until the mushrooms fully absorb the sauce.

Stir in the green beans and eggplants. Cook for 4 to 5 minutes, until the vegetables are tender. Adjust the seasonings to taste. Serve hot.

Fresh Fruit Molds

Gulaman

Serves 6

Southeast Asia is abundant with fresh tropical fruits all year round. Most desserts and other sweet indulgences are considered special treats; instead of eating them after meals they are eaten as snacks between meals. One of the most popular fruits is mango, and Filipino mangoes are sweet and delicious, with many varieties. Any of your favorite fruits can be incorporated into this dish to create a variety of flavors and colors. Filipinos use a seaweed-based gelatin called agar to jell fresh fruits (see page 13). Although the mold can jell without refrigeration, it is best when served thoroughly chilled.

¾ ounce agar powder

6 cups water

1½ cups fresh strawberries, washed and hulled

3 cups granulated sugar, more or less to taste

1½ cups chopped ripe mango flesh

1¾ cups coconut cream

⅛ teaspoon salt, or more to taste

1 cup mixed fruits (such as mixed fresh berries), for decoration

Thoroughly combine the agar powder with the water in a pot over medium heat. Bring to a boil. Decrease the heat and simmer, stirring occasionally, for 2 to 3 minutes, until the agar has completely dissolved. Remove from the heat and strain through a fine sieve. Divide into three equal portions, pouring each portion into a separate bowl. Set aside.

Put the strawberries in a food processor. Add 1 cup of the sugar. Process until well blended. Strain through a fine sieve. Pour most of the strawberry mixture into one of the bowls with the agar, mixing thoroughly (save a little of the strawberry mixture for decoration). Repeat the process with the mango and another cup of sugar (saving a little of the mango mixture for decoration), and pour it into the second bowl of agar.

Stir the coconut cream, the remaining cup of sugar, and salt into the last bowl of agar and mix well.

Pour each bowl of the agar mixture into separate flat-bottomed, 8-inch square pans (such as baking pans) and refrigerate for at least 30 minutes, until set and cold.

To serve, cut the fruit jell into equal-sized shapes, such as diamonds or triangles. Arrange the jell in a decorative pattern on a large serving platter or on individual plates. Decorate with the reserved strawberry and mango mixtures and the mixed fruits. Serve cold.

Note: In cold weather, agar can set very fast at room temperature. Be prepared by making the fruit blends ahead of time, before you boil the agar.

Hot-and-Sour Soup
Sinigang Na Hipon

Serves 6

Southeast Asian menus feature one or more types of hot-and-sour soup as their cultural signature dish, and they are all equally popular and delicious. The "hot" in the soup comes from chiles, and a variety of chiles are available in these climactically suitable regions. The "sour" comes from a variety of possible ingredients, including lime, lemon, tamarind, or various types of vinegars, depending on what is available locally. Filipinos prefer tamarind, which is unique in that it has both a strong flavor and a sour taste. Tamarind pulp is sold in the dry goods section of Asian grocery stores. Tamarind liquid and concentrate are also conveniently available. Serve this soup with steamed rice on the side.

See photo facing page 112.

6 cups vegetable stock

4 to 5 thin slices peeled fresh ginger

1/2 pound firm tofu, well drained and diced

1/2 pound sweet potato, peeled and diced

1/2 pound daikon or jicama, peeled and diced

1/4 pound green beans, cut into 1-inch-long sticks

1 small yellow onion, peeled and cut into 6 to 8 wedges

2 medium tomatoes, cut into 12 wedges

1 bunch watercress or baby spinach, washed and trimmed

1/2 cup tamarind liquid, or more to taste

3 tablespoons light soy sauce

2 red jalape–o or serrano chiles, seeded and chopped

1 tablespoon sugar, or more to taste

1 tablespoon vegetable base (flavor enhancer or bouillon cube)

Salt, to taste

Bring the vegetable stock and ginger to a boil in a large pot over medium heat. Add the tofu, sweet potato, daikon, green beans, and onion. Simmer for 5 to 6 minutes, skimming off any foam or impurities that float to the surface, until the vegetables are almost done.

Add the remaining ingredients, and cook for 2 to 3 minutes longer. Adjust the seasonings to taste. Serve immediately.

Pancit Noodles
Pancit Guisado

Serves 6

In the Philippines, the general word for noodles is pancit, and then a prefix or suffix is added to differentiate the particular noodle dish. The term pancit *derives from the Chinese Hokkien* pianesit, *which means "something that is conveniently cooked." In Filipino cooking, Chinese influences come first, followed by Spanish influences, as in* guisado, *which means "sauté." So, roughly translated, this dish is sautéed noodles with vegetables.*

If using fresh noodles, separate them loosely so they are not in clumps. If using dried noodles, soak them in warm water for 20 to 30 minutes, or until pliable. Drain.

Heat the oil in a wok over medium heat. Add the onion, garlic, ginger, and chiles and cook and stir for 3 to 5 minutes, until light brown and fragrant. Stir in the tofu, carrots, cabbage, and mushrooms. Cook and stir for 2 to 3 minutes, until almost tender.

Increase the heat to high and stir in the noodles, tossing gently until they are evenly combined with the vegetables. Add the vegetable stock, soy sauce, stir-fry sauce, sugar, optional fermented bean curds, and vegetable base. Cook and stir for 3 to 5 minutes, until the noodles are tender. Add more vegetable stock or water, if necessary, and continue cooking until the noodles are thoroughly done. Adjust the seasonings to taste.

Just before removing the wok from the heat, stir in the garlic chives and green onions. Transfer to a serving platter. Sprinkle with the ground pepper and garnish with the bell peppers.

8 to 10 ounces fresh pancit or rice noodles, or 4 to 5 ounces dried noodles

3 tablespoons vegetable oil

1 cup chopped yellow onion

3 tablespoons minced garlic

2 tablespoons peeled and minced fresh ginger

2 tablespoons minced red chiles, more or less to taste

2 cups julienned pressed or firm tofu

2 cups julienned carrots

2 cups thinly sliced green or napa cabbage

2 cups thinly sliced mushrooms of your choice

$^1/_2$ cup vegetable stock or water, plus more as needed

2 tablespoons light soy sauce

2 tablespoons vegetarian stir-fry sauce

2 tablespoons sugar, or more to taste

1 tablespoon fermented bean curds (optional)

1 tablespoon vegetable base (flavor enhancer or bouillon cube)

$^1/_2$ cup sliced Chinese garlic chives, cut into 1-inch-long pieces

$^1/_2$ cup sliced green onions, both green and white parts, cut into 1-inch-long pieces

$^1/_2$ teaspoon ground pepper, for garnish

$^1/_2$ cup julienned red or colorful bell peppers, for garnish

Sweet-Potato Fritters

Ukoy

Serves 6

These deep-fried fritters are best served right out of the pan for optimum crunchiness. When frying the fritters, make sure that each one is thin and flat so the hot oil can get through all the ingredients and create the desired crunchy texture.

To make the batter, peel the sweet potatoes and grate into fine strips using a box grater or hand grater.

Bring the vegetable stock to a boil in a small pot. Place the bean sprouts in a large mixing bowl. Pour the boiling stock over the bean sprouts and let cool to lukewarm.

Add the remaining ingredients to the bowl and stir to mix well. The consistency should be a little thicker than pancake batter; add more vegetable stock or flour as needed.

To make the sauce, combine the vinegar, garlic, chiles, salt, and pepper in a bowl. Stir to mix well. Transfer to a saucer.

To fry the fritters, heat the oil to 375 degrees F in a wok or deep pan. The oil should have the depth of at least 2 inches. Dip a large spoon or ladle into the oil so the oil thinly coats the spoon. Then scoop out the batter and gently slide it into the hot oil. Avoid placing the fritters too close together; the hot oil should bubble between each fritter. Continue the process until the fritters fit loosely in the pan. Fry the fritters for 4 to 6 minutes, ladling them with the hot oil and turning them once, until they are cooked through and are golden brown on both sides. Transfer the fritters to a rack or absorbent paper to drain the oil. Serve the fritters warm, with the sauce on the side.

Batter

1 pound sweet potatoes

1 cup vegetable stock, plus more as needed

1/4 pound bean sprouts

1/2 pound silken tofu, well drained and crumbled

1 cup all-purpose flour

1/2 cup rice flour

1/4 cup cornstarch

1/4 cup thinly sliced green onions, both green and white parts

3 tablespoons minced garlic

2 tablespoons sugar

1 tablespoon vegetable base (flavor enhancer or bouillon cube)

1 teaspoon baking powder

1 teaspoon salt

Sauce and Frying Oil

1/2 cup rice vinegar

2 tablespoons minced garlic

1 tablespoon minced red chiles (optional)

1 teaspoon salt

1/8 teaspoon ground pepper

3 cups vegetable oil

Stir-Fried Noodles
Pancit Bihon Guisado

Serves 6

This is another Chinese-influenced local noodle dish with a Spanish cooking technique. Pancit bihon refers to vermicelli noodles, and guisado means that they are sautéed in the Spanish cooking style. An assortment of vegetables are selected for a variety of tastes, textures, and colors. Choose your favorite noodles and add your favorite vegetables to compose your favorite meal.

Soak the noodles in warm water for 12 to 15 minutes, until soft and pliable. Drain in a colander.

Heat the oil in a pan or wok over medium-high heat. Add the garlic and cook and stir for 1 to 2 minutes, until light brown and fragrant. Add the onion and celery and cook and stir for 2 to 3 minutes, until the onion is translucent.

Add the mushrooms, carrot, bell peppers, and cabbage. Stir to mix thoroughly. Sprinkle with the soy sauce, sugar, stir-fry sauce, and vegetable base. Cook and stir for 2 to 3 minutes.

Toss in the noodles and sprinkle with the vegetable stock, making sure that the noodles are distributed evenly and not clumped together. Continue cooking and tossing for 4 to 5 minutes, until the liquid is absorbed and the noodles are tender. Add more stock or water, if necessary, and continue cooking until the noodles are thoroughly tender. Adjust the seasonings to taste.

Transfer to a serving platter. Sprinkle with the pepper and garnish with the green onions and cilantro. Serve hot, with the lemon wedges on the side.

6 ounces dried rice vermicelli (or, for less carbohydrate, use bean thread vermicelli)

3 tablespoons vegetable oil

3 tablespoons minced garlic

1 cup thinly sliced yellow onion

1 cup thinly sliced Chinese celery or regular celery

1 cup thinly sliced shiitake mushrooms

1 cup matchstick-sliced carrot

1 cup matchstick-sliced colorful bell peppers

1 cup matchstick-sliced cabbage

2 tablespoons light soy sauce

2 tablespoons sugar, or more to taste

1 tablespoon vegetarian stir-fry sauce or seasoned soy sauce

1 tablespoon vegetable base (flavor enhancer or bouillon cube)

1/2 cup vegetable stock, plus more as needed

1/2 teaspoon ground pepper, for garnish

1/4 cup thinly slice green onions, both green and white parts, for garnish

1/4 cup thinly sliced fresh cilantro leaves, for garnish

1 lemon or lime, cut into 6 wedges

Vegetables in Peanut Sauce
Pipián

Serves 6

Traditional pipián is thick and gluey, similar to a rice porridge. This modified version is lighter and cooked more like a vegetable stew, but it still retains the key ingredient—peanuts. If you make the pipián mild, it can be eaten on its own. Or you can add more seasonings to intensify the flavors and serve the dish with steamed rice or noodles.

Heat the oil in a pot or saucepan over medium heat. Add the onion, shallots, and garlic and cook and stir for 4 to 5 minutes, until light brown and fragrant. Stir in the vegetable stock, peanuts, tamarind liquid, paprika, turmeric, and pepper. Bring to a boil, decrease the heat, and simmer for 2 to 3 minutes, stirring frequently so the peanuts don't burn on the bottom of the pot.

Stir in the tofu, carrot, potatoes, jicama, cabbage, soy sauce, sugar, vegetable base, and salt to taste. Cook for 7 to 10 minutes, until the vegetables are tender. Adjust the seasonings to taste. Serve hot.

3 tablespoons vegetable oil

1 cup chopped yellow onion

3 tablespoons minced shallots

2 tablespoons minced garlic

3 cups vegetable stock

1/3 cup ground roasted peanuts or peanut butter

3 tablespoons tamarind liquid or lemon juice, or more to taste

1 tablespoon paprika

1 teaspoon ground turmeric

1/2 teaspoon ground white pepper

1 cup diced firm or fried tofu

1 cup diced carrot

1 cup diced potatoes or pumpkin

1 cup peeled and diced jicama or daikon

1 cup chopped Chinese pickled cabbage or green cabbage

2 tablespoons light soy sauce

2 tablespoons sugar, or more to taste

1 tablespoon vegetable base (flavor enhancer or bouillon cube)

Salt, to taste

Vegetable Adobo
Adobong

Serves 6

There are no Filipino dishes more recognized and celebrated than adobo. And there are so many versions, depending on the key ingredient used and the little tweaks different cooks employ. Invented during the Filipino colonial era, adobo was introduced by the Spanish as a way to preserve food with vinegar. Locals have taken it further by simmering it with herbs and seasonings and reducing it to a thick sauce with intense flavor. The adobo is then served with plain steamed rice or noodles to equalize its intensity.

1 cup distilled or rice vinegar

1/4 cup light soy sauce

1/4 cup chopped garlic

1/4 cup chopped shallots

2 bay leaves

2 tablespoons sugar, or more to taste

1 tablespoon vegetable base (flavor enhancer or bouillon cube)

1/2 teaspoon salt

1/2 teaspoon ground pepper

6 large shiitake mushrooms, tough stems removed

1/2 pound fried tofu, diced

1/2 pound Asian eggplants, cut diagonally into 1-inch-thick pieces

1/2 pound carrots, peeled and diced

1 cup vegetable stock, plus more as needed

Combine the vinegar, soy sauce, garlic, shallots, bay leaves, sugar, vegetable base, salt, and pepper in a pot over medium heat. Bring to a boil. Add the mushrooms, tofu, eggplants, carrots, and vegetable stock. The liquid should cover all of the ingredients in the pot; if it does not, add more stock.

Bring the mixture to a boil again. Decrease the heat to low and simmer for 6 to 8 minutes, until the vegetables are tender. Do not overcook the vegetables or they will fall apart.

With a slotted spoon, remove the solid ingredients and set them aside. Increase the heat to high and bring the liquid to a boil. Simmer for 8 to 10 minutes, until the liquid is reduced by half and forms a thin sauce. Adjust the seasonings to taste.

Return the vegetables to the sauce. Stir to mix well and heat through. Transfer to a serving platter. Serve hot.

Singapore

Sweet-and-Sour Plate
Peal Wan Puk

Serves 6

Sweet-and-sour dishes are popular among Westerners, as these flavors are familiar and comforting. This is also the reason that sweet-and-sour dishes are ordered more than others in Chinese restaurants in the United States. The origin of this Singaporean stir-fry dish is obviously Chinese, with local Southeast Asian touches added. The levels of sweet and sour can be adjusted according to the cook's preference. The sweet-and-sour tastes can also be obtained through various condiments instead of sugar and vinegar.

See photo facing page 152.

2 tablespoons light soy sauce, or more to taste

2 tablespoons vegetarian or mushroom stir-fry sauce

1/3 cup sweet chile sauce, honey, or other syrup, or more to taste

3 tablespoons rice vinegar, or more to taste

2 tablespoons sugar, or more to taste

2 tablespoons cornstarch

1 tablespoon tomato paste (for red color; optional)

1 tablespoon *sambal oelek* (Indonesian hot chile sauce) or sriracha sauce (optional)

1 small orange, zest and juice

3 tablespoons vegetable oil

2 cups julienned fried tofu (3/4 to 1 pound)

3 tablespoons minced garlic

1 cup finely diced water chestnuts

1 cup finely diced onion

1 cup finely diced pineapple or apple

1 cup finely diced colorful bell peppers

Salt and ground pepper, to taste

1/2 cup roasted cashew nuts (optional)

1/2 cup sliced green onions, both green and white parts, cut into 1-inch-long strips

4 sprigs fresh cilantro, leaves only, for garnish

Combine the soy sauce, stir-fry sauce, sweet chile sauce, vinegar, sugar, cornstarch, optional tomato paste, optional *sambal oelek*, and orange zest and juice in a small bowl. Stir to mix well. Set aside.

Heat the oil in a wok over high heat. Add the tofu and cook for 2 to 3 minutes, until light brown and crispy all over. Add the garlic and cook and stir for 1 to 2 minutes. Stir in the water chestnuts, onion, pineapple, and bell peppers. Cook and stir for 2 to 3 minutes. Sprinkle with salt and pepper to taste. Remove the mixture from the wok and set aside.

In the same wok, stir in the soy sauce mixture. Cook and stir for 2 to 5 minutes, until the sauce thickens into a gravy. It should be thick enough to coat the back of a spoon. Add a little water if the sauce is too thick or too dry. Adjust the seasonings to taste.

Stir in the reserved tofu mixture and toss to coat evenly with the gravy. Just before removing from the heat, stir in the cashew nuts and green onions.

Transfer to a serving platter. Garnish with the cilantro.

Fresh Spring Rolls
Poa Pia

Serves 6

In Southeast Asian cuisine, fresh spring rolls are equally as popular as fried spring rolls; Thai and Vietnamese each have their own scrumptious versions. Singapore is a harbor nation where people from all over have consorted. Three major races—Chinese, Malay, and Indian—occupy the land, and Singaporean food is composed of various elements from these original cuisines. Walking along the open-air street hawkers, you will find a Chinese food stall next to a Malay or Indian food stall, or you'll see one that has a combination of the cuisines in a fusion dish.

To make the filling, heat the oil in a wok or pan over medium heat. Add the shallots and garlic and cook and stir for 1 to 2 minutes, until light brown and fragrant. Stir in the cabbage, carrot, jicama, and bamboo shoots. Cook and stir for 2 to 3 minutes, until the vegetables are almost tender. Sprinkle with the soy sauce, sugar, vinegar, vegetable base, and ground pepper. Continue cooking for 2 to 3 minutes, until the vegetables are crisp-tender. Transfer to a serving platter.

Arrange the cucumber, bell peppers, green onions, cilantro leaves, and chiles on a serving platter and serve with the filling.

For self-service, lay 1 wrapper on a plate and scatter about 2 tablespoons of the filling over the lower portion of the wrapper. Top with a small amount of the cucumber, bell peppers, green onions, cilantro, and chiles. Add a dab of hoisin sauce and/or sriracha sauce to taste. Roll up the wrapper from the bottom and wrap the filling tightly to form a log. When the wrap is rolled halfway, fold in both side ends of the wrapper to enclose the filling and continue rolling to completely seal. Eat the roll with your hands.

3 tablespoons vegetable oil

3 tablespoons thinly sliced shallots

2 tablespoons chopped garlic

2 cups matchstick-sliced green or white cabbage

1 cup matchstick-sliced carrot

1 cup peeled and matchstick-sliced jicama or water chestnuts

1 cup matchstick-sliced bamboo shoots

2 tablespoons light soy sauce or seasoning soy sauce (such as Maggi Seasoning Sauce or mushroom-flavored soy sauce)

1 tablespoon sugar, or more to taste

1 tablespoon rice vinegar

1 tablespoon vegetable base (flavor enhancer or bouillon cube)

1/2 teaspoon ground pepper

1 package lumpia wrappers, thawed if frozen

2 cups matchstick-sliced hothouse cucumber

1 cup matchstick-sliced colorful bell peppers

1 cup thinly sliced green onions, both green and white parts

1 cup cilantro leaves

1/4 cup seeded and matchstick-sliced jalape–o or serrano chiles

1 bottle hoisin sauce, as a condiment

1 bottle sriracha sauce or hot mustard, as a condiment

Pickled Shallot-and-Ginger Salad
Yu Sang

Serves 6

The majority of people in Singapore are Chinese; the rest of the population consists mostly of Malay and then Indian. Not surprisingly, Chinese New Year is the largest celebration in Singapore, and all the stops are pulled out. Food is a major part of this event, and this particular dish is dubbed the Chinese New Year salad. Pickled vegetables can be made from scratch or purchased in jars for authentic sweet, tangy, and crunchy elements.

To make the tofu and marinade, combine all the ingredients in a mixing bowl. Marinate in the refrigerator for 10 to 15 minutes.

To make the dressing, combine all the ingredients in a small bowl. Stir to mix well, until the sugar is dissolved.

To make the salad, thinly slice the pickled shallots, ginger, and tea melons. Transfer to a mixing bowl. Add all the remaining ingredients. Toss until well combined.

To serve, combine the marinated tofu and salad mixture. Sprinkle with some of the dressing and toss. Taste and add more dressing as desired. Transfer to a serving platter. Serve immediately.

Tofu and Marinade

1 pound julienned pressed or firm tofu
3 tablespoons peeled and matchstick-sliced fresh ginger
1 tablespoon light soy sauce
1 tablespoon freshly squeezed lemon or lime juice
1 teaspoon sesame oil
1/4 teaspoon ground white pepper

Dressing

1/2 cup Chinese white plum sauce (ready-made in a jar)
1/4 cup water
2 tablespoons freshly squeezed lemon or lime juice
1 tablespoon light soy sauce or seasoning soy sauce (such as Maggi Seasoning Sauce or mushroom-flavored soy sauce)
1 tablespoon sugar, or more to taste
1/4 teaspoon salt, or more to taste

Pickled Ingredients and Salad

5 to 6 Chinese pickled shallots (ready-made in a jar) or shallots soaked in seasoned rice vinegar for 5 to 7 days
1/2 cup pickled ginger (ready-made in a jar) or peeled and sliced fresh ginger soaked in seasoned rice vinegar for 5 to 7 days
3 to 4 Chinese pickled tea melons (ready-made in a jar)
2 cups peeled and matchstick-sliced daikon or jicama
2 cups matchstick-sliced carrots
1/2 cup whole fresh cilantro leaves
5 to 6 fresh kaffir lime leaves, very thinly sliced (chiffonade)
1/4 cup thinly sliced green onions, both green and white parts
1/4 cup coarsely chopped roasted peanuts
2 tablespoons roasted black and white sesame seeds

Ripe Papaya Salad

Yum Pawpaw

Serves 6

Papaya grows abundantly in the tropical climate of South-east Asia. Many varieties of papaya have been cultivated on large-scale plantations, producing sweet papaya for eating as a fruit, green papaya for eating as a vegetable, and medicinal papaya for healing various ailments. For multiple colors and textures, combine different types of papaya in this dish. Ripe papaya flesh is very delicate, so be as gentle as possible when handling it and tossing the salad ingredients.

To prepare the fruits and vegetables, peel and seed the papaya and gently slice it into thin strips. Be careful not to bruise the flesh. Peel and slice the jicama into thin strips. If using the avocado and mango, gently peel and seed them and slice the flesh into thin strips.

Arrange the salad greens in serving bowls and top with the papaya, jicama, optional mango, and optional avocado. Refrigerate to chill.

To make the dressing, combine all the ingredients in a bowl. Stir to mix well.

Just before serving, sprinkle the salad with the dressing and garnish with the sesame seeds. Serve chilled.

Fruits and Vegetables

1 small, ripe Hawaiian papaya, or 3 cups other papaya flesh
1 medium jicama
1 large, ripe mango (optional)
1 large, ripe avocado (optional)
1/4 pound assorted baby salad greens
1 tablespoon roasted sesame seeds, for garnish

Dressing

1/4 cup thinly sliced green onions, both green and white parts
2 tablespoons light soy sauce
2 tablespoons freshly squeezed lime juice, or more to taste
1 tablespoon vegetable oil
1 tablespoon sugar
1 tablespoon minced chiles, more or less to taste
1 teaspoon sesame oil

Stuffed Flat Bread
Martabak

Serves 6

Indian culture and cuisine are a big part of Singapore, the hot spot of Southeast Asia. Martabak has its origin in southeast India in the state of Tamil Nadu, where the majority of the people are Tamils, as are most of the Indians residing in Singapore. For this recipe, Indian bread called roti is filled with a mild curry stuffing. In Singapore, the process of handling roti has become a theatrical art form; a vendor has to create a performance out of rolling, tossing, and stretching the dough before filling it with a delicious stuffing.

Bread

3½ cups all-purpose flour, plus more for kneading

1 tablespoon sugar

1 teaspoon salt

⅓ cup vegetable oil, plus more for kneading

1⅓ cups lukewarm soymilk

To make the bread, sift the flour, sugar, and salt together in a mixing bowl. Stir in the vegetable oil and mix thoroughly, until crumbly. Gradually stir in the soymilk to form a soft, sticky dough.

Dust a flat work surface with flour and knead the dough for 10 to 12 minutes, dusting it with more flour as needed, to form a smooth ball. Put the dough back in the bowl and cover with a damp towel. Let the dough rest in a warm place for 30 to 45 minutes.

Lightly oil a flat work surface and roll the dough into a long cylinder. Cut the dough into 8 equal pieces. Roll each piece into a ball. Arrange the balls, not touching each other, on a lightly oiled tray. Cover with the damp towel. Let the dough rest for 3 to 4 hours.

Oil the work surface, your hands, and/or a rolling pin. Spread and flatten each ball of dough, stretching it into a thin round, 6 to 8 inches in diameter. Spread about ¼ cup of the filling (page 133) in the center of the round to make a 4- to 5-inch circle. Fold the edges of the dough from 4 sides and overlap them in the middle, covering the filling completely and forming a 5- to 6-inch-square envelope. Continue making more envelopes with the dough and filling.

Apply some oil to thinly coat a large pan or griddle over medium heat. The oil should be hot enough to be almost smoking. Place the envelopes in the pan to fit loosely and cook for 3 to 4 minutes, until the bottom is golden brown. Turn the envelopes over and cook the other side until golden brown. Transfer to a platter and keep warm.

To make the filling, heat the oil in a pan over medium heat. Add the garlic, ginger, and chiles and cook and stir for 2 to 3 minutes, until light brown and fragrant. Stir in the remaining ingredients and cook and stir for 6 to 8 minutes, until the vegetables are tender. Adjust the seasonings to taste. Let cool before stuffing the dough.

To serve, cut the flat breads into small pieces. Serve warm.

Filling

3 tablespoons vegetable oil

3 tablespoons minced garlic

3 tablespoons peeled and minced fresh ginger

1 tablespoon minced chiles (optional)

1 cup chopped yellow onion

1 cup green peas

1 cup finely diced carrot

2 tablespoons Indian curry powder

2 tablespoons very thinly sliced (chiffonade) fresh curry leaves (optional)

2 tablespoons sugar

1 tablespoon vegetable base (flavor enhancer or bouillon cube)

1 teaspoon salt

Yellow Noodles
Mee Hokkein

Serves 6

Singapore and Malaysia are close neighbors, and the Malay people are the second largest group in Singapore after the Chinese. Malaysians also have their own version of this recipe using the same Chinese Hokkien yellow noodles. Little tweaks of local preference have been added to make this delicious noodle dish as different as their language.

Separate the fresh noodles so they are not clumped together. If using dried noodles, soak them in warm water for 15 to 20 minutes, until pliable, and then drain.

Heat the oil in a wok over medium-high heat. Add the garlic and ginger and cook and stir for 1 to 2 minutes, until light brown and fragrant.

Increase the heat to high and add the onion, mushrooms, snow peas, bell peppers, and tofu. Cook and stir for 2 minutes, until everything is well mixed. Toss in the noodles and mix well, making sure the noodles are not clumped together.

Sprinkle with the vegetable stock, soy sauce, stir-fry sauce, sugar, rice wine, and vegetable base. Toss to mix well. Cook until all liquid has been absorbed and the noodles are tender, adding more stock or water, if necessary. Adjust the seasonings to taste.

Just before removing from the heat, stir in the bean sprouts and garlic chives. Stir and toss to combine well. Transfer to a serving platter and sprinkle with the ground pepper. Serve the noodles hot, with the lemon wedges on the side.

8 to 10 ounces fresh Hokkein yellow noodles, or 4 to 5 ounces dried Hokkein yellow noodles

3 tablespoons vegetable oil

3 tablespoons minced garlic

2 tablespoons peeled and minced fresh ginger

1 cup thinly sliced yellow onion

1 cup thinly sliced shiitake mushrooms or mushrooms of your choice

1 cup matchstick-sliced snow peas

1 cup julienned colorful bell peppers

1 cup julienned pressed or firm tofu

1/2 cup vegetable stock, plus more as needed

2 tablespoons light soy sauce

2 tablespoons vegetarian stir-fry sauce

2 tablespoons sugar, or more to taste

2 tablespoons rice wine or sherry

1 tablespoon vegetable base (flavor enhancer or bouillon cube)

1/4 pound beans sprouts

20 fresh garlic chives, or 2 stalks green onion, cut into 1 1/2-inch-long strips

1/2 teaspoon ground white pepper

1 lemon or lime, cut into 6 wedges

Sri Lanka

Okra Curry
Bandakka Curry

Serves 6

Okra is a choice vegetable that originated in Africa but is used much more exclusively in the Middle East, India, and Sri Lanka. In America, okra most often appears in the gumbo soups featured in Creole cookery. Young okra is preferred for this recipe. With only a quick fry, it will retain its crunchy texture, or you can cook it slowly in the sauce to bring out its soft and characteristically gummy texture.

To prepare the okra, combine it with the turmeric, chile powder, and salt in a mixing bowl. Toss to mix well.

Heat the oil in a pan or wok over medium heat. Fry the okra in small batches for 2 to 3 minutes, until cooked but crunchy. Drain on absorbent paper. Set aside.

To make the sauce, add the onion to the oil remaining in the pan or wok used to fry the okra, and cook and stir over medium heat for 2 to 3 minutes, until light brown and fragrant. Add the chiles, coriander, cumin, cinnamon stick, curry leaves, and salt. Stir in the coconut milk and decrease the heat to low. Simmer for 10 minutes. Adjust the seasonings to taste.

For crispy okra, serve the sauce on the side. For soft okra, toss the okra in the pan with the sauce and serve immediately.

Okra

1 pound young okra, trimmed and thinly sliced crosswise

1 teaspoon ground turmeric

1 teaspoon chile powder or paprika

1/2 teaspoon salt

1/2 cup vegetable oil

Curry Sauce

1 cup chopped yellow onion

3 tablespoons minced green jalape–o or serrano chiles, more or less to taste

2 teaspoons ground coriander

1 teaspoon ground cumin

1 cinnamon stick

5 to 6 fresh or dried curry leaves or bay leaves

1 teaspoon salt

1 cup coconut milk

Pickled Eggplants
Vambotu Pahi

Serves 6

This pickled eggplant is similar to Indian chutney, but Sri Lankans add more spices to glorify and distinguish it as the hot southern region's cookery. The amount of spices, especially chiles, can be adjusted to your taste. Refrigerating the eggplant in a tightly sealed jar will help it keep for several weeks. Serve it the traditional way, as a side dish, or use it to accompany curries, as you would a chutney. Alternatively, it makes a tasty filling for sandwiches.

4 to 6 Asian long purple eggplants (about 2 pounds)
1 tablespoon salt, or more to taste
3/4 cup vegetable oil, plus more as needed
3 tablespoons chopped shallots
2 tablespoons chopped garlic
2 tablespoons chopped green jalape–o or serrano chiles, more or less to taste
1 tablespoon black mustard seeds
2 teaspoons ground coriander
1 teaspoon ground cumin
1 teaspoon ground fennel
1 teaspoon ground turmeric
1/2 teaspoon chile powder
1/2 cup water
1/4 cup tamarind liquid or rice vinegar
1 tablespoon sugar, or more to taste

Slice the eggplants in half lengthwise. Cut the halves crosswise into 1/4-inch-thick pieces. Rub the sliced eggplant thoroughly with the salt and let rest in a colander for at least 1 hour. Rinse with cold running water. Let dry in the colander or pat dry with paper towels.

Heat a little of the oil in a skillet or wok over medium heat. Fry the eggplant (in small batches so it cooks evenly) for 3 to 4 minutes. Transfer to a plate and set aside.

Add a little more of the oil to the skillet and stir in the shallots, garlic, and chiles. Cook for 1 to 2 minutes, until light brown and fragrant. Stir in the mustard seeds, coriander, cumin, fennel, turmeric, and chile powder. Cook and stir for 1 to 2 minutes. Stir in the water, tamarind liquid, and sugar. Cook and stir for 3 to 4 minutes, until the mixture turns into a thin gravy.

Return the eggplant to the skillet, along with any liquid. Stir gently to mix well. Cook for 6 to 8 minutes. Adjust the seasonings to taste. Remove from the heat and let cool.

Transfer the eggplant to jars with airtight lids. Store in the refrigerator for up to 4 weeks.

Spiced Coconut Custard
Vatalapan

Serves 6

Every Asian country has its own version of a custard dessert, with various influences from different Western countries. For example, Thai custard, sangkaya, was adapted from a Portuguese dessert from the sixteenth century; Vietnamese flan has a French influence; and Sri Lankan custard probably evolved from one or all of these cultures: Portuguese, Dutch, and English. Custard recipes have been modified with substitutions of native ingredients, adding local sensibilities and enhancing flavors to fit restricted palates. Coconut cream and coconut milk play a key role in making Asian creamy desserts because dairy cream and milk are hard to find. Local fragrances, such as jasmine or pandan, replace vanilla or lavender.

1¼ cups palm or light brown sugar

2 pandan leaves, or ½ teaspoon pandan or jasmine extract

1¾ cups coconut cream (one 14-ounce can)

1 cup silken tofu, well drained

3 tablespoons cornstarch

¼ teaspoon ground cinnamon

¼ teaspoon ground cardamom

¼ teaspoon ground cloves

¼ teaspoon ground nutmeg

¼ teaspoon ground fennel or your choice of spice

Combine the sugar, pandan leaves or extract, and ¼ cup of water in a small pot over medium heat. Stir for 2 to 3 minutes until the sugar is melted and the mixture turns into a thin syrup.

Move the oven rack to the center of the oven. Preheat the oven to 375 degrees F.

Combine the coconut cream, tofu, and cornstarch in a mixing bowl. Whisk gently until well blended. Beat in the syrup, cinnamon, cardamom, cloves, nutmeg, and ·fennel. Remove and discard the pandan leaves, if using.

Distribute the mixture among 6 to 8 small ramekins. Arrange the ramekins in a heatproof pan with at least 2-inch-high edges. Pour warm or hot water into the pan so the water reaches halfway up the sides of the ramekins.

Carefully place the pan in the center of the oven rack.

Bake for 15 to 20 minutes, until the custard is firm without jiggling in the center when gently shaken.

Remove from the oven and let cool. Run a thin, small blade around the inside rim of each ramekin. Turn the ramekins upside down onto serving plates, and then remove the ramekins. Serve the custard warm or cold.

Thailand

Coconut-and-Banana Ice Cream
I-tim Ma Prow

Serves 6

Common in Thai neighborhoods are traveling wheel-cart vendors ringing their bells to sell coconut ice cream. They offer freshly made ice cream with various toppings: roasted nuts, fruits, or sweet, sticky rice. Ice cream can be served in a variety of ways: in a cup, in a cone, or in a hollowed-out, four-inch-long baguette for a hearty snack. This recipe adds banana for a special touch. Fresh fruits of your choice can be incorporated. Freshly made coconut cream or milk is preferable for a refreshing coconut taste. (See page 27 for how to make fresh coconut milk.)

3 very ripe bananas, peeled

2 teaspoons freshly squeezed lemon or lime juice

5 cups coconut cream (preferably freshly made from fresh, mature coconut flakes)

1½ to 2 cups superfine sugar

Mash the bananas in a mixing bowl. Add the lemon juice and mix well. Add the coconut cream and sugar and whisk until well incorporated.

Transfer the mixture to an ice-cream maker and freeze according to the manufacturer's instructions. Alternatively, pour the mixture into a freezer-safe container and freeze for 8 to 12 hours until solidly firm.

Sweet Crêpes with Bananas
Khuay Haw Thong

Serves 6

Influences from foreign countries intertwine in modern Thai cookery. Burgers and crêpes are now a part of the Thai daily diet. The younger generations in Thailand know more about pizzas and milkshakes than curry and palm toddy drinks.

To make the crepes, combine all the ingredients in a mixing bowl. Gently whisk into a smooth batter.

Heat a thin coat of oil in a medium-sized, nonstick pan or skillet over medium heat until almost smoking. Stir the batter and ladle about 1/3 cup into the pan. Tilt the pan so the batter spreads to cover the pan's surface. Cook for 1 to 2 minutes, until the crêpe is dry and set on top. Flip the crêpe and cook the other side for 1 to 2 minutes. Transfer to a plate. Continue the process to make more crêpes.

To serve, stuff the crêpes with the banana filling and fold each crêpe into a roll, a cone, or an envelope.

To serve with fresh and cold banana filling, gently toss the bananas with the lemon juice in a bowl. Fill the crêpes with the bananas and drizzle with the honey and coconut cream. Serve with nondairy whipped cream, if desired.

To serve with warm banana filling, combine the bananas, lemon juice, honey, and coconut cream in a pot over medium heat. Cook, stirring gently, for 2 to 3 minutes, until heated through. Fill the crêpes with the warm bananas. Serve with nondairy whipped cream, if desired.

Crêpes

1 1/2 cups all-purpose flour

1 1/2 cups water

1/4 cup cornstarch

1/4 cup coconut milk

1 lemon, zest only

2 tablespoons brown sugar

1/2 teaspoon salt

1/2 teaspoon ground turmeric

Banana Filling

6 ripe bananas, peeled and sliced into thin, bite-sized pieces

1 lemon, juiced (use the same lemon used for the zest in the crêpe batter)

1/4 cup honey or corn syrup, or more to taste

3 tablespoons coconut cream

Nondairy whipped cream (optional)

Green Curry Patties
Thod Mun

Serves 6

Thod mun *is a deep-fried dish that is popular as a snack at hawker stores throughout Thailand. Its main spice comes from Thai curry paste, which is conveniently available ready-made in a jar. Traditionally, Thai red curry paste was used, giving the patties a reddish color. But any Thai curry paste is now acceptable, so greenish and yellowish colors with different spices from Thai green and yellow curry pastes are the new varieties of* thod mun. *To get a more or less intense flavor of curry, just adjust the amount of curry paste in the recipe.*

1 pound silken tofu, well drained

3 tablespoons cornstarch

1½ tablespoons Thai green curry paste, more or less to taste

1 tablespoon sugar

1 tablespoon light soy sauce

1 tablespoon vegetable base (flavor enhancer or bouillon cube)

2 large, fresh kaffir lime leaves, very thinly sliced (chiffonade)

1 cup thinly sliced green beans or long beans (sliced crosswise into small circles)

1 large red chile, seeded and chopped (optional)

3 tablespoons chopped fresh cilantro leaves

3 cups vegetable oil, for frying

Combine the tofu, cornstarch, green curry paste, sugar, soy sauce, vegetable base, and kaffir lime leaves in a food processor. Pulse several times until well blended.

Scrape the mixture into a mixing bowl. Fold in the green beans, optional chile, and cilantro. Mix thoroughly.

With dampened hands, shape the mixture into small patties, about 1½ inches in diameter. Lightly oil a tray and arrange the patties on it in a single layer.

Heat the oil in a deep pan or a wok to 375 degrees F. The oil should have a depth of at least 2 inches. Make sure that the oil is hot before adding the patties. Drop the patties into the pan to fit loosely. Fry for 3 to 5 minutes, turning once or twice, until golden brown all over. Drain on a rack or on absorbent paper. Serve the patties with Cucumber Dipping Sauce (page 143) on the side.

To make the dipping sauce, combine the sugar, water, vinegar, and salt in a small pot over medium heat. Bring to a boil and cook for 2 minutes, until the mixture turns into a thin syrup. Remove from the heat and let cool.

Just before serving, transfer the syrup to a bowl and add the cucumber, carrot, bell pepper, and optional peanuts.

Cucumber Dipping Sauce

1/3 cup sugar

1/4 cup water

1/4 cup rice vinegar

1 teaspoon salt

3 cups thinly sliced cucumber, cut into half-moons

1/2 cup matchstick-sliced carrot

1/2 cup matchstick-sliced colorful bell peppers

1/4 cup chopped roasted peanuts (optional)

Grilled Bananas
Khuay Ping

Serves 6

Thai bananas come in many varieties: short, skinny, long, round, green, yellow, and red. Their textures are similar but their flavors are almost as different as night and day. The long, yellow, and highly fragrant bananas (Cavendish) commonly found in the United State have recently become popular in Thailand; they were dubbed khuay hom, *which means "fragrant banana" in Thai. For different tastes, a variety of bananas should be used, but take into consideration their ripeness and cooking time. Some bananas, if they are fully ripe, fall apart very easily when cooked.*

6 bananas, not fully ripe

1 lime, zest and juice

1 tablespoon finely chopped kaffir lime skin (zest) or very thinly sliced (chiffonade) fresh kaffir lime leaves (optional)

1/2 cup dried sweetened coconut flakes

1 cup nondairy whipped cream

1/4 cup coconut cream

1 tablespoon vegetable oil

1/4 cup honey (optional)

Slice the bananas into 3-inch-long, 1/2-inch-thick pieces. Toss the bananas with the lime zest and juice and the optional kaffir lime skin.

Toast the coconut flakes in a dry pan over medium heat, stirring frequently, for 4 to 5 minutes, until light brown and fragrant. Alternatively, preheat the oven to 350 degrees F. Put the coconut flakes in a pan and roast them in the oven for 7 to 10 minutes, until golden brown. Set aside.

Combine the whipped cream and coconut cream and whisk until lightly firm. Set aside.

Heat a grill pan over medium heat. Lightly coat the pan with the oil. Grill the bananas for 3 to 4 minutes, turning once, until tender, cooked through, and lightly charred brown.

Transfer the bananas to a serving platter. Sprinkle with the optional honey and the toasted coconut. Serve with the whipped cream mixture.

Roasted Spicy Pineapple

Suparod Ob

Serves 6

Tropical fruits make this recipe a standout and more authentic. If tropical fruits are hard to come by in your area, seasonal fruits with textures similar to pineapple and mango can be used. An apple is a convenient substitute; although the dish will taste vaguely similar to apple strudel, kaffir lime will add a little touch of Thai.

1 pineapple, peeled and cored
1 mango, peeled and pitted
1 star fruit
1 orange, zest and juice
1/3 cup coconut cream
1/3 cup honey or corn syrup
1/4 cup brown sugar
1 teaspoon ground cinnamon
1 teaspoon grated nutmeg
1 tablespoon kaffir lime skin (zest) or very thinly sliced (chiffonade) fresh kaffir lime leaves (optional)
1 cup nondairy whipped cream
2 ripe passion fruits

Preheat the oven to 400 degrees F.

Slice the pineapple and mango flesh into 1-inch cubes. Cut the star fruit in half lengthwise and remove the seeds. Slice it into 1-inch-thick pieces. Set aside.

Combine the orange juice, coconut cream, honey, sugar, cinnamon, and nutmeg in a large pot over medium heat. Cook for 2 to 3 minutes, stirring constantly, until the sugar is completely dissolved. Add the fruits and optional kaffir lime skin to the pot. Stir to combine well.

Pour the mixture into a roasting pan and place in the oven. Roast for 25 to 30 minutes, until the fruits are lightly browned and cooked through. Remove from the oven.

Combine the orange zest with the whipped cream in a bowl and set aside.

Before serving, cut the passion fruits in half and squeeze the flesh and seeds over the roasted fruits. Serve the fruits with the whipped cream.

Simple Mixed-Vegetable Salad
Yum Puk

Serves 6

See photo facing page 153.

The vegetables in this recipe can be stir-fried, poached, or steamed for a healthful preparation without oil. Any favorite vegetables of your choice can be used. The salad can be served warm, at room temperature, or cold if the vegetables and dressing are chilled in the refrigerator before mixing.

To prepare the vegetables, heat the oil in a pan or wok over medium heat. Add the chiles and cook and stir for 1 to 2 minutes, until dark brown and crispy. Remove from the oil and set aside. Add the onion, ginger, and garlic to the pan and cook and stir for 2 to 3 minutes, until light brown and fragrant.

Stir in the carrots, broccoli, red and yellow bell pepper, snow peas, and baby corn and cook and stir for 2 to 3 minutes, until tender, adding little water if needed. (The vegetables can be poached or steamed until tender without oil, if you prefer. If you poach or steam them, the chiles, ginger, and garlic can be mixed in with the dressing.)

To make the dressing, combine all the ingredients in a bowl. Mix well.

Transfer the vegetables to a serving platter and sprinkle with the dressing. Garnish with the basil leaves just before serving.

Vegetables

2 tablespoons vegetable oil

3 dried small chiles

1 cup chopped yellow onion

2 tablespoons peeled and minced ginger

1 tablespoon minced garlic

1½ cups julienned carrots

1½ cups small broccoli florets

1 cup julienned red bell pepper

1 cup julienned yellow bell pepper

1 cup snow peas, trimmed and cut in half lengthwise

1 cup baby corn or asparagus, cut in half lengthwise into 1½-inch-long strips

¼ cup very thinly sliced (chiffonade) Thai sweet basil leaves, for garnish

Dressing

3 tablespoons light soy sauce, or more to taste

3 tablespoons freshly squeezed lime juice

2 tablespoons rice vinegar

2 tablespoons sugar, or more to taste

1 teaspoon minced Thai chiles, more or less to taste

Salt, to taste

Asian Fusion

Spicy Noodle Soup
Guay Tiaw Gaeng

Serves 6

During centuries of trading with Thailand, China brought noodles and India brought curry. The Thai people have taken the best of both, creating many curried noodle dishes. Different areas, from the north through the south of Thailand, have a curried noodle dish that is considered a regional specialty. Each region adds a local touch, a one-of-a-kind ingredient, and has a unique technique as its signature. This recipe is a collective result, with elements from all the regions combined. Ready-made curry paste is used, and any type is acceptable—red, green, or yellow. For a creamer curry sauce, replace the vegetable stock with coconut milk.

4 ounces dried rice vermicelli noodles

1 cup vegetable oil

1/4 cup thinly sliced shallots

3 tablespoons minced garlic

3 slices peeled fresh ginger

2 cups firm tofu, well drained and diced

2 cups thinly sliced shiitake mushrooms

2 tablespoons Thai curry paste (green, red, or yellow)

4 to 5 cups vegetable stock or coconut milk

2 tablespoons sweet soy sauce

2 tablespoons light soy sauce

3/4 teaspoon ground black pepper

3 tablespoons chopped fresh cilantro, for garnish

3 tablespoons chopped green onion, for garnish

Soak 3 ounces of the noodles in warm water for 5 to 10 minutes and then drain. Heat the oil in a wok or saucepan over medium heat until almost smoking (375 degrees F). Make sure that the oil is hot enough before proceeding. Sprinkle the remaining ounce of noodles in the hot oil. Cook for 15 to 20 seconds, until the noodles are fully puffed and have turned bright white. With tongs or a strainer, transfer the puffed noodles to absorbent paper to drain. Set aside for garnish.

Remove all but 2 tablespoons of the oil from the wok. Stir in the shallots, garlic, and ginger and cook and stir for 1 to 2 minutes, until light brown and fragrant. Add the tofu, mushrooms, and curry paste and cook and stir for 2 to 3 minutes.

Add the vegetable stock and bring to a boil. Stir in the soaked noodles, sweet soy sauce, light soy sauce, and pepper. Simmer for 3 to 5 minutes, until the noodles have swelled and are fully cooked. Adjust the seasonings to taste.

Distribute the noodles, vegetables, and sauce among serving bowls and garnish with the fried noodles, cilantro, and green onion. Serve immediately, before the noodles swell and become mushy.

Stir-Fried Curried Mushrooms
Pad Hed Krueng Gaeng

Serves 6

After the first rain of the season in Thailand, a variety of mushrooms pop up overnight like fully heated popcorn. In some places, the ground is literally covered with white dots. Fortunately, in any season here, cultivated exotic mushrooms pop up regularly on local grocery store shelves. Mixed varieties of mushrooms cut in a uniform size make a great combination of tastes and textures. For just the glory of mushrooms, stir-fry them without curry paste. For a special touch, Thai curry paste will add another dimension of delicate flavors. Serve this dish with steamed rice or cooked noodles.

H eat the oil in a wok over high heat. Add the curry paste and cook for 1 to 2 minutes, until fragrant. Add all the mushrooms and cook and stir for 1 to 2 minutes, until tender.

Add the remaining ingredients. Cook and stir for 1 to 2 minutes, until combined and heated through. Transfer to a serving platter. Serve immediately.

3 tablespoons vegetable oil

2 tablespoons Thai curry paste (green, red, or yellow)

1 cup (4 ounces) thinly sliced shiitake mushrooms

1 cup (4 ounces) thinly sliced oyster mushrooms

1 cup (4 ounces) thinly sliced abalone mushrooms

1 cup (4 ounces) thinly sliced mushrooms of your choice

1 cup (6 ounces) peeled and thinly sliced water chestnuts or jicama

1 cup (2 ounces) bean sprouts

1/4 cup thinly sliced green onions

2 tablespoons light soy sauce or seasoning soy sauce (such as Maggi Seasoning Sauce or mushroom-flavored soy sauce), or more to taste

2 tablespoons sweet soy sauce

1 tablespoon palm or brown sugar, or more to taste

1 tablespoon vegetable base (flavor enhancer or bouillon cube)

Yellow Fried Rice with Crispy Shallots
Kao Pad Pong Garee

Serves 6

There are fried-rice recipes in this book from all over Asia, and this last one is from Thailand. The basic ingredients are almost the same, except for the little touches that make each one unique. And for Thai fried rice, curry powder is the key. Curry powder in the market comes in many varieties; some have intense flavor and are very spicy, such as Indian and Madras curry powders, and some are mild and used only for imparting a yellow color, such as Chinese curry powder.

¼ cup vegetable oil

¾ cup very thinly sliced shallots

2 tablespoons minced garlic

1 tablespoon minced Thai chiles, more or less to taste

2 cups thinly sliced mushrooms of your choice

1 cup snow peas or green beans, trimmed and cut into thin strips

1 cup baby corn or peeled and sliced jicama, cut into thin strips

1 cup julienned colorful bell peppers

3 cups cooked or steamed rice (prepared from 1½ cups uncooked rice), or 3 cups chilled leftover rice, crumbled

2 tablespoons light soy sauce

2 tablespoons seasoning soy sauce (such as Maggi Seasoning Sauce or mushroom-flavored soy sauce)

2 tablespoons vegetarian stir-fry or mushroom stir-fry sauce

2 tablespoons sugar, or more to taste

1 tablespoon vegetable base (flavor enhancer or bouillon cube)

1 tablespoon curry powder

1 cup roasted cashew nuts (optional)

Heat the oil in a wok over medium heat. Add the shallots and cook and stir for 2 to 3 minutes, until light brown and fragrant, taking care that they do not burn. Drain on absorbent paper. Set aside for garnish.

Increase the heat to high and add the garlic and chiles to the remaining oil in the wok. Cook and stir for 2 to 3 minutes, until light brown and fragrant. Add the mushrooms, snow peas, baby corn, and bell peppers and cook and stir for 1 to 2 minutes.

Add the rice and mix until evenly distributed. Sprinkle with the sauces, sugar, vegetable base, and curry powder. Cook and stir for 2 to 3 minutes, until well combined, evenly colored, and heated through.

Add the optional cashew nuts and stir to mix well. Adjust the seasonings to taste.

Transfer to a serving platter and sprinkle with the fried shallots. Serve immediately.

Tofu Pockets

Hor Song

Makes 24 pockets; serves 6

This is a modified recipe, converting Chinese fried, stuffed wontons into a Thai snack. Instead of just plain vegetables, Thai spices are added in the form of Thai curry paste, which contains all the Thai herbs (such as lemongrass, galangal, and kaffir lime) and spices (such as cardamom, coriander, and cumin seeds). The amount of liquid in the filling is critical to making a semidry texture for easy stuffing. All excess water in the tofu should be completely drained.

Put the tofu, jicama, green onions, curry paste, lime juice, soy sauce, sugar, salt, and pepper in a bowl and thoroughly combine.

Arrange a piece of wonton skin on a flat surface in a diamond shape. Scoop about 1 tablespoon of the tofu mixture onto the lower corner of the wonton skin. Roll the skin over the mixture, and halfway through, fold both sides of the wrapper on top of the log. Apply a little water on the open end of the wrapper and roll to seal completely. Repeat the process to make more pockets.

Heat the oil in a deep pan or wok to 375 degrees F. The oil should have a depth of at least 2 inches. Make sure that the oil is hot first before lowering the pockets into the pan to fit loosely. Cook for 2 to 3 minutes, turning the pockets occasionally, until golden brown and crispy all over. Remove from the pan. Drain on a rack or absorbent paper.

Serve the pockets with Ginger Syrup Dipping Sauce (page 151) or ready-made Thai sweet chile sauce.

Tofu Pockets

1 pound silken tofu, well drained

1 cup peeled and matchstick-sliced jicama

1/4 cup chopped green onions, both green and white parts

1 to 2 tablespoons Thai red curry paste, or more to taste

2 tablespoons freshly squeezed lime juice

1 tablespoon light soy sauce

1 tablespoon sugar

1/2 teaspoon salt

1/2 teaspoon ground pepper

1 package ready-made wonton skins, cut into 3-inch squares

3 cups vegetable oil, for frying

To make the dipping sauce, combine the sugar, water, and fresh ginger in a small pot over medium heat. Bring to a boil and simmer for 2 to 3 minutes, until the sugar is completely dissolved.

Remove from the heat and add the remaining ingredients. Stir to mix well.

Ginger Syrup Dipping Sauce

⅓ cup sugar

⅓ cup water

3 thin slices peeled fresh ginger

¼ cup minced preserved ginger or pickled ginger in a jar (pink ginger)

3 tablespoons rice vinegar

½ teaspoon salt

Singaporean Sweet-and-Sour Plate (Peal Wan Puk), p. 128

Thai Simple Mixed-Vegetable Salad (Yum Puk), p. 146,
Vietnamese Braised Mushrooms (Nam Xao Nuoc Tuong),
p. 154

Vietnam

Braised Mushrooms
Nam Xao Nuoc Tuong

Serves 6

See photo facing page 153.

This simple mushroom dish makes a great side addition to all fresh salads. It provides salty, earthy flavors from soy sauce and mushrooms, which make a great contrast to refreshing salads. Fresh straw mushrooms are very popular in Vietnam and are best suited for this recipe. Fresh straw mushrooms are difficult to find in the United States, and although canned straw mushrooms in brine are available, their bland flavor and mushy texture diminish the delicious result. Fresh button mushrooms can be used, and their different types can be mixed together for variety.

1½ to 2 pounds small button mushrooms of your choice

2 tablespoons vegetable oil

3 tablespoons chopped garlic

½ cup vegetable stock or water, plus more as needed

3 tablespoons soy sauce or soy sauce mixed with seasoning soy sauce (such as Maggi Seasoning Sauce or mushroom-flavored soy sauce)

2 tablespoons sugar

2 tablespoons garlic-and-bean sauce or spicy bean paste

½ teaspoon cracked pepper, plus more for garnish

Salt, to taste

3 tablespoons chopped cilantro leaves, for garnish

C lean the mushrooms and trim and discard the tough stems. If using a variety of mushrooms, cut them into a uniform size so they cook evenly and are done at the same time.

Heat the oil in a wok or pan over medium heat. Add the garlic and cook and stir for 2 to 3 minutes, until light brown and fragrant. Add the mushrooms and stir briskly to combine well.

Stir in the vegetable stock, soy sauce, sugar, bean sauce, pepper, and salt to taste. Simmer for 7 to 10 minutes, until the mushrooms are tender.

Transfer to a shallow bowl. Garnish with the cilantro and additional cracked pepper.

Chef's Salad
Rau Dron Gein

Serves 6

Chef's salad is prevalent in every cuisine, and all the chefs' creations are equally imaginative. Fresh, local vegetables are preferred to heighten the seasonal taste. Any vegetables of your choice can be substituted for the ones in this recipe, and even seasonal fruits can be used. Arrange the salad ingredients decoratively, and serve the dressing on the side. This is your own chef's salad!

To make the salad, clean and cut all the vegetables uniformly. Refrigerate to chill and keep crispy.

To make the dressing, combine all the ingredients in a small mixing bowl. Stir until the sugar is dissolved.

Just before serving, combine all the ingredients in a mixing bowl. Add the dressing and toss until evenly distributed. Alternatively, arrange the vegetables decoratively on a serving platter (similar to the American chef's salad) and serve with the dressing on the side.

Salad

2 cups thinly sliced iceberg lettuce
1 cup matchstick-sliced carrot
1 cup matchstick-sliced hot house cucumber
1 cup peeled and matchstick-sliced jicama
1 cup matchstick-sliced colorful bell peppers
1 cup bean sprouts
1 cup julienned crunchy fried tofu
¼ cup thinly sliced (chiffonade) fresh mint leaves
¼ cup thinly sliced fresh cilantro leaves

Dressing

1 cup coarsely chopped roasted peanuts
¼ cup freshly squeezed lime juice
¼ cup light soy sauce
1 tablespoon sugar, more or less to taste
1 tablespoon minced garlic, or more to taste
1 teaspoon minced Thai chiles, more or less to taste

Dry Curried Noodles
Bun Cari

Serves 6

Chinese influence has had an effect on everything Vietnamese, and noodles are a good example of this in Vietnamese cuisine. Wet noodles, pho, with plenty of tasty broth are among the most popular; dry noodles are occasionally served to break the monotony. This recipe includes curry powder for an aromatic flavor and a touch of Indian flair. The Chinese also make their own version of curry powder, which is milder in flavor but rather keen on yellow color. For an aromatic punch, use the original and intense Indian curry powder.

To make the noodles, combine the tofu, lemongrass, curry powder, soy sauce, stir-fry sauce, pepper, and cornstarch in a mixing bowl. Set aside to marinate for 10 to 15 minutes.

Heat the oil in a skillet or wok over medium heat. Add the onions and cook and stir for 2 to 3 minutes, until tender.

Stir in the tofu mixture and cook and stir for 2 to 3 minutes, until well combined and heated through. Add the coconut cream, vegetable base, and sugar. Cook and stir for 2 to 3 minutes, until well mixed and heated through. Add salt and additional sugar to taste. Turn off the heat.

Cook the noodles in boiling water until tender (1 to 2 minutes for fresh noodles or 3 to 5 minutes for dried noodles). Drain and rinse with cold water until completely cold.

Noodles

1 pound julienned firm tofu (3 cups)

2 tablespoons very thinly sliced lemongrass, tender midsection only, cut into thin rings

1 tablespoon curry powder, or more to taste

1 tablespoon light soy sauce

1 tablespoon vegetarian stir-fry sauce

1 teaspoon ground pepper

1 teaspoon cornstarch

3 tablespoons vegetable oil

3 cups thinly sliced yellow onions (about 2 large onions)

1/2 cup coconut cream

1 tablespoon vegetable base (flavor enhancer or bouillon cube)

1 tablespoon sugar, more or less to taste

Salt, to taste

8 to 10 ounces fresh vermicelli noodles (any kind), or 4 to 5 ounces pound dried Japanese somen noodles

2 cups bean sprouts, as accompaniment

1 head lettuce, cleaned and cut to bite-sized pieces, as accompaniment

1 bunch fresh cilantro leaves, as accompaniment

1 bunch fresh mint leaves, as accompaniment

1 bunch fresh Thai sweet basil leaves, as accompaniment

1 cup Sweet Chile Sauce, as accompaniment (page 157)

To make the Sweet Chile Sauce, combine the water, sugar, tamarind liquid, garlic, and salt in a small pot and bring to a boil. Cook until the sugar is dissolved. Remove from the heat and let cool.

Just before serving, add the *sambal oelek*. Transfer to a serving bowl and sprinkle with the optional roasted peanuts and carrot.

Distribute the cooked noodles on one side of serving plates and ladle the curried mixture on the other side of the plates. Serve with the vegetables, herbs, and Sweet Chile Sauce on the side.

Sweet Chile Sauce

Makes 1 cup

1/3 cup water

1/4 cup palm or brown sugar

3 tablespoons tamarind liquid or rice vinegar

2 tablespoons minced garlic

1/2 teaspoon salt, or more to taste

1 tablespoon *sambal oelek* (Indonesian hot chile sauce), more or less to taste

2 tablespoons chopped roasted peanuts, for garnish (optional)

2 tablespoons finely shredded carrot, for garnish

Herbed Noodles
Cha Hanoi

Serves 6

Vietnamese cuisine is at the forefront of healthful eating, as it features combinations of cooked and fresh vegetables that are served with a variety of fresh herbs. This recipe has its origin in Hanoi, the old capital city in the north of Vietnam. Across the northern border is China, whose influence in the culinary field is scattered throughout this recipe, beginning with the inclusion of noodles and ending with the cooking technique of wok stir-frying. The final touch, though, is distinctly Vietnamese—fresh herbs and a signature sauce.

Cook the noodles in plenty of boiling water for 4 to 6 minutes, until tender. Drain and rinse with warm running water. Distribute the noodles among serving bowls.

Heat the oil in a wok or pan over medium heat. Add the garlic and ginger and cook and stir for 1 to 2 minutes, until light brown and fragrant.

Stir in the mushrooms, water chestnuts, carrots, and long beans. Cook and stir for 2 to 3 minutes, until the vegetables are partially tender. Sprinkle with the soy sauce, sugar, vegetable base, turmeric, and pepper. Cook and stir for 2 to 3 minutes, until the vegetables are tender. Just before removing from the heat, stir in the green onions, basil, cilantro, mint, dill, and peanuts.

Noodles

4 to 5 ounces dried rice vermicelli noodles or cellophane noodles

3 tablespoons vegetable oil

3 tablespoons chopped garlic

3 tablespoons peeled and chopped fresh ginger

1/4 pound mushrooms of your choice, sliced into thin strips

1/4 pound water chestnuts or jicama, peeled and finely diced

1/4 pound carrots, peeled and finely diced

1/4 pound long beans or green beans, cut into 1 1/2-inch-long strips

2 tablespoons light soy sauce

2 tablespoons sugar

1 tablespoon vegetable base (flavor enhancer or bouillon cube)

1 teaspoon ground turmeric

1/2 teaspoon ground pepper

1 cup matchstick-sliced green onions, both green and white parts

1 cup fresh Thai sweet basil leaves, plus more for serving

1 cup fresh cilantro leaves, plus more for serving

1 cup fresh Vietnamese mint (*rau ram*) or mint leaves, plus more for serving

1 cup fresh dill, plus more for serving

1/2 cup chopped roasted peanuts

1 cup Dipping Sauce (page 159)

1 lime or lemon, cut into 6 wedges

To make the dipping sauce, combine all the ingredients in a bowl. Stir until the sugar is completely dissolved. Distribute among serving saucers.

Distribute the vegetables over the warm noodles in the bowls. Serve the noodles with the Dipping Sauce, lime wedges, and additional fresh herbs.

Dipping Sauce
Nouc Cham

Makes about 1 cup

1/4 cup freshly squeezed lime or lemon juice

1/4 cup light soy sauce

1/4 cup water

3 tablespoons sugar

2 tablespoons minced garlic

1 teaspoon minced red chiles or *sambal oelek* (Indonesian hot chile sauce), more or less to taste

Clay-Pot Eggplant
Qua-Ca Kho To

Serves 6

This dish has a deep, intense, sweet flavor dominated by caramel syrup. It should be served with steamed rice to help dilute the intense flavor. The eggplants absorb the sauce well and become saturated with juicy flavors. Cut the eggplants into a uniform size so they cook evenly and are done at the same time. The longer the eggplants simmer in the syrup, the more intense the flavor and the thicker the sauce will be.

To make the Carmel Soy Syrup, combine all the ingredients in a pot over medium heat. Cook for 10 to 15 minutes, until the mixture is reduced to a thick syrup that coats the back of a spoon. Take care that the mixture does not boil over or burn. While it is cooking, the sauce will give off a very pungent odor. Be prepared and keep the kitchen well ventilated.

Stored in a covered container in the refrigerator, Caramel Soy Syrup (or any leftover syrup) will keep for one month, so you can make it in advance, if you like.

To make the Eggplant, heat the vegetable oil in a medium-sized clay pot or regular pot over medium heat. Stir in the shallots and garlic and cook and stir for 1 to 2 minutes, until light brown and fragrant. Add the eggplants and chiles. Toss to mix well.

Add the Caramel Soy Syrup, stir-fry sauce, vegetable base, rice vinegar, and black pepper. Stir to combine well. Cover and continue cooking over medium-low heat for 7 to 10 minutes, until the eggplants are tender and the liquid is reduced to a thick sauce. Add more Caramel Soy Syrup to taste.

Caramel Soy Syrup
Nuoc Mau-Si Dau

Makes 1/2 to 3/4 cup

1/3 cup finely chopped candy sugar or brown sugar

1/3 cup light soy sauce

3 tablespoons water

Eggplant

2 tablespoons vegetable oil

3 tablespoons minced shallots

3 tablespoons minced garlic

5 to 6 cups (1 1/2 pounds) diced Asian eggplants

6 whole Thai red chiles, bruised to lightly split, more or less to taste

1/2 to 3/4 cup Caramel Soy Syrup

2 tablespoons vegetarian stir-fry sauce or vegetarian oyster sauce

1 tablespoon vegetable base (flavor enhancer or bouillon cube)

1 tablespoon rice vinegar

1 teaspoon ground black pepper

3 tablespoons chopped fresh cilantro leaves, for garnish

1/2 cup matchstick-sliced colorful red bell peppers, for garnish

4 sprigs fresh sweet basil leaves, for accompaniment

4 sprigs fresh mint leaves, for accompaniment

4 sprigs fresh sawtooth herb or Vietnamese mint *rau ram*, for accompaniment

Remove from the heat and sprinkle with the cilantro and bell peppers. Serve the dish with the fresh herbs as accompaniments.

Marinated Lemongrass Tofu
Dou Fu Hyay

Serves 6

Lemongrass is a major herb in Vietnamese cuisine and is used liberally in marinades and sauces. Its sweet, lemony fragrance provides a unique aroma, its crunchy filaments add beneficial fiber to the diet, and its medicinal properties include curing indigestion and aiding the body with antibacterial defenses. Only the tender inner sections of the lemongrass are suitable for eating and adding to marinades and sauces. The tough outer sections are good for infusing flavor into broths and making tea.

To make the marinade and tofu, process the lemongrass, garlic, turmeric, salt, and pepper into a paste in a mortar with pestle or in a food processor.

Slice the tofu into $1/2$-inch-thick slabs, each 2 x 4 inches. Gently toss the tofu with the lemongrass mixture and set aside to marinate for 30 to 60 minutes.

Heat the oil in a pan over medium heat. When the oil is hot, arrange the tofu in it in a single layer to fit loosely. Cook for 3 to 4 minutes, turning once, until light brown. You will need to cook the tofu in several batches, depending on the size of your pan. Transfer the cooked tofu to a serving plate and top with the sauce.

To make the sauce, heat $1/2$ cup of the coconut cream in a pan over medium heat. Stir in the lemongrass and garlic and cook and stir for 3 to 4 minutes, until light brown and fragrant.

Stir in the remaining coconut cream, soy sauce, sugar, and vegetable base and cook for 2 to 3 minutes. Adjust the seasonings to taste.

Marinade and Tofu

$1/3$ cup thinly sliced lemongrass, tender midsection only

2 tablespoons chopped garlic

1 tablespoon ground turmeric

1 teaspoon salt

1 teaspoon ground pepper

2 pounds firm tofu, well drained

$1/4$ cup vegetable oil, for frying

Sauce

$1 3/4$ cups (one 14-ounce can) coconut cream

$1/2$ cup very fine minced lemongrass, tender midsection only

3 tablespoons minced garlic

2 tablespoons light soy sauce

1 tablespoon sugar

1 tablespoon vegetable base (flavor enhancer or bouillon cube)

Marinated Vegetables

Rau Giam

Makes 4 to 5 cups

Marinated, or pickled, vegetables have a special place on the Vietnamese dining table, alongside the fresh vegetables and herbs that are served as accompaniments. These vegetables add zesty, salty, sweet, and tangy flavors to almost every dish, especially Western-style Vietnamese sandwiches and hot dogs, where they function similarly to dill pickles and sauerkraut.

1 cup sugar

$^3/_4$ cup rice or distilled vinegar

$^1/_2$ cup water

1 teaspoon salt

1 large carrot, peeled and julienned (about 2 cups)

1 medium daikon, peeled and julienned (about 2 cups)

1 orange, red, or yellow bell pepper, julienned (about 1 cup)

$^1/_2$ pound pearl onions, peeled (about 1 cup)

6 green and red Thai chiles, or 3 green and red jalape–o chiles, sliced

To make the marinade, combine the sugar, vinegar, water, and salt in a pot and bring to a boil. Simmer for 1 to 2 minutes, until the sugar is dissolved.

Mix the vegetables and chiles and arrange them tightly in a bowl or jar. Pour the still-hot marinade over them, making sure that all the vegetables are submerged (if necessary, make additional marinade). Set aside at room temperature until cool.

Stored in a tightly covered container in the refrigerator, Marinated Vegetables will keep for 1 month.

Bean-Noodle Soup

Gaa Mien

Serves 6

Bean, cellophane, and glass noodles are made from mung beans, and when cooked, they turn glassy clear. Even after being cooked and used in recipes, such as in soups or stir-fries, or mixed with acidic salad dressings, their texture remains firm and elastic without disintegrating, unlike other types of noodles. Their taste and texture are also distinctively different from noodles made from rice or wheat, adding another flavor dimension to Vietnamese noodle dishes.

Soak the noodles in warm water for 10 to 15 minutes, until pliable. Drain and cut the noodles into 6-inch strands. Set aside.

Bring the vegetable stock to a boil in a pot. Add the yellow onions and cook for 10 to 15 minutes, until they almost disintegrate. Strain out the onions and reserve the clear stock.

Return the stock to a boil. Add the noodles, mushrooms, tofu, white onion, carrot, soy sauce, wine, vegetable base, optional sugar, and pepper. Cook for 3 to 4 minutes, until the noodles and vegetables are tender. Adjust the seasonings to taste.

Ladle the soup into serving bowls. Garnish with the green onion and cilantro.

4 ounces dried mung bean, cellophane, or glass noodles

8 cups vegetable stock

2 yellow onions, thinly sliced

1/2 pound shiitake mushrooms, thinly sliced

1/2 pound firm tofu, julienned (optional)

1 white onion, thinly sliced

1 carrot, peeled and cut crosswise into thin rounds

2 tablespoons light soy sauce, or more to taste

2 tablespoons Shaoxing rice wine or sweet sherry

1 tablespoon vegetable base (flavor enhancer or bouillon cube)

1 tablespoon sugar (optional)

1/2 teaspoon ground white pepper

3 tablespoons chopped green onion, both green and white parts, for garnish

3 tablespoons chopped fresh cilantro leaves, for garnish

Stewed Vegetables in Coconut Juice
Dua Hu Heo Kho Nuos Dua

Serves 6

Young, green coconut is a popular fresh fruit. Its fresh juice can easily quench your thirst, and its tender, white meat satisfies as a snack. Its fragrant, sweet juice is often used as a base or broth in various Vietnamese stews. Many Asian grocery stores carry fresh, whole young coconuts in their produce aisles; frozen coconut juice and meat are sold in plastic packages in the frozen foods section. Serve this dish with steamed rice.

To make the Caramel Syrup, combine the sugar and cool water in a pot and bring to a boil. Do not stir. Decrease the heat to medium and cook for 10 to 12 minutes. When the syrup turns dark brown and the bubbles become sluggish, remove from the heat and slowly add the $1/4$ cup of hot water. Watch out, as it will splash!

Increase the heat to high and cook for 3 to 5 minutes longer. Stir in the lemon juice and remove from the heat.

Caramel Syrup
Nuoc Mau

Makes $1/2$ to $3/4$ cup

Caramel Syrup and any leftover syrup can be stored in a covered container in the refrigerator for up to a month.

1 cup sugar, candy sugar, or brown sugar

$1/4$ cup cool water

$1/4$ cup hot water

2 tablespoons freshly squeezed lemon or lime juice

For the fresh coconut, use a heavy clever to chop off the top of the coconut, and then pour the juice into a bowl. With a long-handled spoon, scoop out the tender, white meat of the coconut and mix it with the juice.

Heat the oil in saucepan or wok over medium heat. Add the lemongrass, shallots, and garlic, and cook and stir for 2 to 3 minutes, until light brown and fragrant.

Add the tofu, water chestnuts, lotus roots, Caramel Syrup, soy sauce, five-spice powder, and pepper. Cook, stirring occasionally, for 2 to 3 minutes.

Add the coconut meat, coconut juice, and vegetable stock. Bring to a boil. Skim off any foam or impurities that float to the surface. Decrease the heat to medium-low and simmer for 20 to 30 minutes, until everything is tender. Add more Caramel Syrup to taste.

Transfer to a shallow bowl and garnish with the cilantro. Serve hot.

Vegetables

1 whole young coconut, or 2 cups frozen coconut juice and meat

2 tablespoons vegetable oil

1/2 cup minced lemongrass, tender midsection only (2 to 3 stalks)

3 tablespoons chopped shallots

2 tablespoons chopped garlic

3/4 pound fried spongy tofu, diced

1 1/2 cups peeled and finely diced water chestnuts or jicama

1 1/2 cups peeled and thinly sliced lotus roots (about 1/2 pound)

1/2 to 3/4 cup Caramel Syrup

1/3 cup light soy sauce, or more to taste

1 teaspoon Chinese five-spice powder, or more to taste

1 teaspoon ground black pepper

1 cup vegetable stock

3 sprigs fresh cilantro, leaves only, for garnish

Stuffed Zucchini
Yoi Gaar

Serves 6

This recipe takes a little time and requires some skill to stuff the zucchini tightly so that after it is cooked and sliced for serving the stuffing won't fall apart. Slice the stuffing ingredients into thin, small pieces, as this will help them to bind with the tofu. You can either steam or fry the stuffed zucchini. Each method provides different delicious results: soft and moist with steaming and lightly crunchy with frying.

To prepare the zucchini, trim both ends of the zucchini and hollow out the seeds. If the zucchini are very long, cut them in half crosswise and hollow out the seeds. Set aside.

Squeeze as much water out of the soaked mushrooms as possible and thinly slice them into matchsticks.

To make the stuffing, combine the tofu, mushrooms, and all of the remaining stuffing ingredients. Mix thoroughly.

Fill the cavities of the zucchini tightly with the stuffing. Use a chopstick or rod to help push the stuffing in firmly.

To steam the stuffed zucchini, place them in a steamer insert. Steam over boiling water for 8 to 10 minutes, until the zucchini are tender and the stuffing is firm and cooked through. Test by poking with a fork.

To deep-fry the stuffed zucchini, heat 3 cups of oil in a deep pan over medium heat to 375 degrees F; the oil should have a depth of at least 2 inches. Gently lower the stuffed zucchini into the hot oil and fry for 6 to 8 minutes,

Zucchini and Stuffing

6 large green and/or yellow zucchini

6 to 8 dried black mushrooms, soaked for 10 to 15 minutes in water until soft

1 pound soft tofu, well drained and crumbled

1 carrot, shredded (about 1 cup)

3 tablespoons thinly sliced green onion, both green and white parts

2 tablespoons cornstarch

1 tablespoon light soy sauce

1 tablespoon vegetarian mushroom or stir-fry sauce

1 tablespoon vegetable base (flavor enhancer or bouillon cube)

1 tablespoon sugar

1 teaspoon ground pepper

Accompaniments

1 cup Nouc Cham Sauce (page 167)

4 cups Vietnamese Marinated Vegetables (page 162)

1 bunch fresh cilantro

1 bunch fresh mint

1 bunch fresh Thai sweet basil

until the zucchini are tender and the stuffing is firm and cooked through. Test by poking with a fork. Drain on a rack or absorbent paper.

Arrange all the accompaniments in bowls and plates.

To make the Nouc Cham Sauce, combine the water, sugar, vinegar, garlic, chile, and salt in a small pot and bring to a boil. Simmer for 1 to 2 minutes, or until the sugar is dissolved. Remove from the heat and let cool.

Just before serving, transfer to a serving bowl and sprinkle with the optional roasted peanuts and carrot.

To serve the stuffed zucchini, slice crosswise into $^1/_2$-inch-thick pieces and arrange on a serving platter. Serve with accompaniments.

Nouc Cham Sauce

Makes 1 cup

$^1/_3$ cup water

$^1/_4$ cup sugar

3 tablespoons rice vinegar

2 tablespoons minced garlic

1 tablespoon minced red chile or *sambal oelek* (Indonesian hot chile sauce), more or less to taste

$^1/_2$ teaspoon salt, or more to taste

2 tablespoons chopped roasted peanuts, for garnish (optional)

2 tablespoons finely shredded carrot, for garnish

Stuffed Baguette
Gun Kajoa

Serves 6

French-style patisseries are as common as local grocery stores in Vietnamese marketplaces. French baguettes are essential to Vietnamese breakfasts and quick lunches. Stuffed baguette sandwiches are popular fast meals and are served in as many ways as their Western-sandwich counterparts. This version has been modified to use only plant-based ingredients.

To make the stuffing, heat the oil in a skillet over medium heat. Add the shallots and cook and stir for 1 to 2 minutes, until light brown and fragrant. Stir in the tomatoes and tofu and cook for 2 to 3 minutes, until well incorporated.

Stir in the soy sauce, sugar, vegetable base, and pepper. Cook until all the liquid has evaporated; the texture should be fairly dry. Remove from the heat and stir in the green onion and cilantro.

Cut each baguette crosswise into 6 to 8 pieces, and then slice lengthwise, keeping one side attached, to make sandwich buns. Spoon the stuffing into the baguettes and top with the lettuce, vegetables, and herbs.

Stuffing

3 tablespoons vegetable oil

1/4 cup chopped shallots

1 pound ripe tomatoes, chopped

1 pound firm tofu, finely chopped

2 tablespoons light soy sauce

2 tablespoons sugar

1 tablespoon vegetable base (flavor enhancer or bouillon cube)

1 teaspoon ground pepper

3 tablespoons chopped green onion, both green and white parts

3 tablespoons chopped fresh cilantro leaves

Accompaniments

2 fresh baguettes

1 head lettuce, leaves separated

2 cups Vietnamese Marinated Vegetables (page 162; optional)

1 cup fresh Thai sweet basil leaves

1 cup fresh mint leaves or other fresh herbs of your choice

Resources

Aiemsabuy, Oopchaeal. *Tofu Aroi, Delicious Tofu*. Bangkok: Sangdad Books, 1997.

Davidson, Alan. *The Penguin Companion to Food*. New York: Penguin Group, 2002.

Gruenwald, Joerg. *PDR for Herbal Medicines*. Montcale: Medical Economic Company Inc., 1998.

Herbst, Sharon Tyler. *The New Food Lover's Companion*. New York: Barron's Educational Series, Inc., 2001.

Hlengmaharnaka, Vanida. *Arharn Vietnam*, Bangkok: Sangdad Books, 2000.

Holzen, Heinz von. *The Food of Asia*. Singapore: Periplus Editions (HK) Ltd., 1999.

Jue, Joyce. *Asian Appetizers*. Emeryville: Harlow & Ratner, 1991.

Jue Joyce. *Savoring Southeast Asia*. San Francisco: A Weldon Owen Production, 2000.

Kazumo, Emi. *Japanese Cooking*. London: Hermes House, 2003.

Kongpun, Sisamon. *The Best of Vegetable Dishes*. Bangkok: Sangdad Books, 2000.

Mahidol University. *The Miracle of Veggies 108*. Bangkok: Kopfai Publishing, 1997.

Megal, Christophe. *Asian Tapas*. Hong Kong: Periplus Editions, 2005.

Mingkwan, Chat. *The Best of Regional Thai Cuisine*. New York: Hippocrene Books, 2002.

Mingkwan, Chat. *Buddha's Table: Thai Feasting Vegetarian Style.* Summertown, TN: Book Publishing Company, 2004.

Mingkwan, Chat. *Vietnamese Fusion: Vegetarian Cuisine.* Summertown, TN: Book Publishing Company, 2007.

Mcnair, James. *Cooks Southeast Asia.* San Francisco: Chronicle Books, 1996.

Mowe, Rosalind, ed. *Southeast Asian Specialties.* Cologne: Konemann, 1998.

Owen, Sri. *Classic Asian.* London: DK Publishing Inc., 1998.

Parragon Books Ltd. *The Asian Cookbook.* Bath: Parragon Publishing Book, 2006.

Poladitmontri, Panurat. *The Thai Beautiful Cookbook.* San Francisco: Collins Publishers, 1992.

Thonanong, Thongyao. *Royal Court Recipes.* Bangkok: Sangdad Books, 1998.

Trieu, Thi Choi. *The Food of Vietnam.* Singapore: Periplus Editions (HK) Ltd., 1998.

Walden, Hilary. *The Encyclopedia of Creative Cuisine.* London: Quarto Publishing Limited, 1986.

Online Suppliers

Ingredients for making Asian food at home can be found in local Asian markets or grocery stores. You also can conveniently shop on the internet. Just type "Asian ingredients" into a search engine and you'll find many websites and online retailers devoted to Asian foods and ingredients. Here are a few good places to start:

Local Asian Markets
www.newasiancuisine.com

Online Retailers
www.importfood.com
www.pacificgourmet.com
www.templeofthai.com
www.vietworldkitchen.com
www.diamondorganics.com

Asian Fusion

About the Author

As the youngest boy in an urban family in Bangkok, Chat Mingkwan was often left behind to help his aunt prepare the family dinner while his older brothers and sisters ran off to play. At first he despised the task of cooking, but he later learned to enjoy the knowledge and skills he gained, including discovering the sweet revenge of spiking and overspicing his brother's and sisters' meals. Chat often intentionally prepared their meals with almost unbearable spiciness and got away with it. The food was so spicy but still so delicious that Chat's siblings were unsure whether to punish or praise him. Eventually cooking became his passion. He gradually fine-tuned his skills and continued cooking, although praise was his only reward and encouragement.

Chat came to the United States to pursue higher education in a design field, while cooking and training part-time in a French restaurant as a hobby. This was his first big step in the culinary profession. With a degree from California State University, Chat worked for several years in the hospitality design business, specializing in kitchen and restaurant design. Later he followed his yearning culinary passion by apprenticing at La Cagouille in provincial French cuisine in Rayon, France. Returning to the United States, he offered his French cooking always with a twist of Asian, and perfected his Asian cooking with a hint of French techniques to fit the Western kitchen. Chat traveled extensively throughout Southeast Asia and realized a wealth of culinary knowledge among these countries and within their unique cuisine. He again became an apprentice, this time of Southeast Asian cuisine, and easily mastered the skill with his Thai cooking background. Chat put his skills to the test for several years in the culinary metropolis of San Francisco at a restaurant that specialized in Southeast Asian grilled food, before realizing his call of sharing the knowledge. He later traveled again, this time through Asia at large, tasting and learning the native cuisine of each Asian country and understanding their relationship to each other. He's now doing what he likes most: cooking, teaching, traveling, writing, and making sure that people who come in contact with him have a full stomach and a good time.

Chat's overall philosophy is similar to his cooking—simplicity. Untie the knot, either the one in your stomach or the unclear one in the recipe. Make it simple, straightforward, and true to yourself. Chat invites you to walk with him on this path.

Visit Chat at www.unusualtouch.com.

Index

Recipe titles appear in **bold** typeface.

BOOK PUBLISHING COMPANY

since 1974—books that educate, inspire, and empower

To find your favorite vegetarian and soyfood products online, visit:
www.healthy-eating.com

more great books from Chat Mingkwan

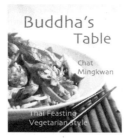

Buddha's Table
978-1-57067-161-6

Vietnamese Fusion
978-1-57067-207-1

Japanese Cooking:
Contemporary & Traditional
Miyoko N. Schinner
978-1-57067-072-5

The New Now & Zen Epicure
Miyoko N. Schinner
978-1-57067-114-2

Authentic Chinese Cuisine:
For the Contemporary Kitchen
Bryanna C. Grogan
978-1-57067-101-2

Purchase these vegetarian cookbooks from your local bookstore or natural foods store,
or you can buy them directly from:
Book Publishing Company • P.O. Box 99 • Summertown, TN 38483 • 1-800-695-2241
Please include $3.95 per book for shipping and handling.